P9-CKD-253

Careers for You Series

McGraw-Hill's

CAREERS FOR

BOOKWORMS

& Other Literary Types

MARJORIE EBERTS
MARGARET GISLER

FOURTH EDITION

New York   Chicago   San Francisco   Lisbon   London   Madrid   Mexico City
Milan   New Delhi   San Juan   Seoul   Singapore   Sydney   Toronto

The *McGraw·Hill* Companies

Library of Congress Cataloging-in-Publication Data

Eberts, Marjorie.
    Careers for bookworms & other literary types / by Marjorie Eberts & Margaret
    Gisler — 4th ed.
        p.   cm.   — (McGraw-Hill careers for you series)
    Includes bibliographic references.
    ISBN-13: 978-0-07-154539-6 (alk. paper)
    ISBN-10: 0-07-154539-5 (alk. paper)
    1. Book industries and trade—Vocational guidance—United States. 2.
    Publishers and publishing—Vocational guidance—United States. 3.
    Information science—Vocational guidance—United States. 4. Library
    Science—Vocational guidance—United States. 5. Research—Vocational
    guidance—United States. I. Gisler, Margaret. II. Title. III. Title: Careers for
    bookworms and other literary types.

Z471.E25 2008
381'45002023—dc22   2008024669

1 2 3 4 5 6 7 8 9 10 11 12 13 14 15 16 17 18 19 20 DOC/DOC 0 9 8

ISBN 978-0-07-154539-6
MHID   0-07-154539-5

McGraw-Hill books are available at special quantity discounts to use as premiums
and sales promotions or for use in corporate training programs. To contact a
representative, please visit the Contact Us pages at www.mhprofessional.com.

This book is printed on acid-free paper.

To Patty White, our favorite bookworm,
who reads books, hoards books,
and keeps them as friends forever

WITHDRAWN

Contents

Acknowledgments

W e wish to thank the many bookworms who shared personal stories of careers that truly let them read on the job. We also want to thank the following people, who provided timely career information:

Jenifer Grady   American Library Association
Valerie Hawkins   American Library Association
Lisa Hendrickson   Oxbridge Communications
Tina Jordan   Association of American Publishers, Inc.
Brenda Shields   Canadian Library Association

CHAPTER ONE

Careers for Bookworms

Investigating the Opportunities

I n 1815, Thomas Jefferson wrote in a letter to John Adams, "I cannot live without books." Today, bookworm bloggers are commenting online: "I've never met a bookstore that I didn't like." "I do not understand the concept of being too busy to read." "I'll read anything—even the back of a ketchup bottle." "I have more bookshelf space than floor space." They are also going online to display their book collections to fellow cybersurfers. And one of the great benefits of the Internet is the websites that let bookworms find fellow book aficionados who direct them to even more books to read. This is a golden age for bookworms. Never before have there been so many printed materials to read. In North America, you have the choice of more than 1.5 million titles in print. Plus, there are actually billions of opportunities to read online materials, from newspapers to magazines to encyclopedias to government documents to the websites themselves, with their diverse information. And many bookworms now enjoy reading e-books on a variety of new devices.

While being a bookworm today might peg you as a member of a relatively small group of people, many young children are likely to join you in the future. They have recently discovered the magic of reading—in large part through the Harry Potter series. Their enthusiasm even extends at times to eschewing television for reading.

It is not difficult to recognize fellow bookworms. They are the ones with their noses buried in books on buses and planes. They read while eating a solitary lunch in a cafeteria. They read at swimming pools, on park benches, and even in front of television sets. Libraries and bookstores are their second homes. Wherever there are books, there will be bookworms close by.

Bookworms are entranced by great literature, captivated by mysteries, enthralled by biographies, fascinated by histories, attracted to nonfiction, and drawn to all books, from encyclopedias to bestsellers. The longer bookworms live with books, the more the magnetism of books draws them into reading more and more titles. They are the most educated people on earth.

A Bookworm's Perfect Job

You will be delighted to know that your love of the printed page can lead to a career in which having to read at work is a qualification for many jobs. If you see yourself reading from nine to five every day, start looking at all the ads in newspapers and magazines and on websites to find that special job that will let you do even more reading. Read the ads carefully, and you will find appealing jobs like these:

JUNIOR REFERENCE LIBRARIAN—FEDERAL GOVERNMENT

DUTIES
- Provide information and documentation
- Compile and update reading lists

QUALIFICATIONS
- Master's degree in library sciences or library and information sciences
- Knowledge of reference sources, printed and in various electronic formats, and of official government publications

---

- Knowledge of online searching techniques and of the major commercial database systems
- Knowledge of current affairs

ASSOCIATE EDITOR—TRAVEL MAGAZINE

Description: Candidates should have previous magazine experience. Must be willing to travel and attend evening events. Must be able to handle multiple responsibilities simultaneously. Must be able to turn in quality work on tight monthly deadlines.

Requirements: Strong editing and proofreading skills required. Knowledge of or interest in travel.

BOOK REVIEWER—TRADE MAGAZINE

Description: Seeking experienced reviewers in the nonfiction areas of house and home improvement, gardening, cooking, entertaining, and parenting. Must be able to demonstrate the following with published clips: grammatically expert and straightforward writing style; extensive knowledge of subject matter in which you indicate interest.

Requirements: Please note the subcategories within nonfiction in which you can demonstrate your strongest suits. Show through clips and a very detailed cover letter how you can back up your claims.

STORY ANALYST—MAJOR HOLLYWOOD STUDIO

Description: Must have experience in reading scripts and writing coverages. Must have excellent command of grammar and easy-to-read writing style.

Requirements: Must be union story analyst. Must be willing to work on studio lot. Must be able to work full-time.

A Brief Look at Job Possibilities

Several years ago, a confirmed bookworm was browsing through the first edition of this book hoping to find a job that involved substantial amounts of reading. When she chanced to read the section on special libraries, she immediately knew that this was the place where she wanted to work. Today, this bookworm is happily reading on the job as deputy manager in the research department of the library at *BusinessWeek* magazine. In Chapter 2, you will read about how she got this job and how much reading she is fortunate to do at work every day. We hope this book will help you discover a job that will let you be paid for reading. Here is a bird's-eye view of some of the jobs you will read about in this book.

Library Careers

A librarian's career is one where you get to hang out with books on the job. You also get to share your workday with fellow bookworms because almost every librarian is a bookworm. Besides books, today's libraries have the most advanced media, from the Internet to virtual libraries. The main job of librarians remains the same as it was in the past, however: to collect, organize, and make information available to people. The difference is that they now use technology to handle much of their work. They also have the opportunity to work in a wide variety of settings. You will find librarians working at such places as law offices, newspapers, magazines, and even zoos.

Book Publishing Careers

More than two hundred thousand books are being published each year in North America by more than eighty thousand publishing houses—resulting in many jobs in this area for bookworms. The job is especially appealing because jobs like editor, proofreader, indexer, and book critic present opportunities to do a lot of reading on the job. Book publishing companies come in all sizes. You could work in a large publishing house, like the one that published this book, or a small one with just a few employees. Because so many bookworms want to be involved in the process of creating books, there is considerable competition for publishing jobs. The easiest way to get your foot in the door at these companies is by working as an intern or taking any kind of entry-level position.

Magazine and Newspaper Careers

Bookworms do not just bury their noses in books. They read anything that is printed, especially magazines and newspapers. Today, they are also reading the online versions of these publications. The Internet has opened up more job possibilities for bookworms. Although many of the editorial jobs in magazines and newspapers are similar to those in book publishing, there are several additional jobs. Think about all the letters magazines and newspapers receive; someone has to read them and handle them appropriately. Then research must be done to ensure that everything that is printed is accurate and that reporters have all the background information needed for their articles. Within this variety, several jobs offer bookworms the opportunity to do nothing but read.

Internet Career Opportunities

Bookworms will always have a passion for books and the printed page. Today, however, they sometimes leave the world of print to read their beloved books sitting in front of a computer or while using such things as a cell phone or handheld electronic reader. When you are thinking of a career that will let you read for a great part of the day on the job, don't forget to consider looking at jobs associated with the Internet. Many new and interesting careers are evolving that are perfect for bookworms, from being an indexer or abstractor to developing a website that will attract bookworms.

Glamorous Reading Careers

Bookworms are not just fascinated by the printed word. Many are drawn to jobs in the movie industry, television, radio, and public relations that offer a touch of glamour. A few find careers in front of a microphone or camera. Most work behind the scenes. After all, someone has to be hired to screen scripts to discover the right properties for a movie studio or television show and to handle a superstar's mail. And behind every talk-show host on radio and television, there is usually a producer reading like crazy to find topics that will grab an audience. A few of these jobs require working closely with stars, especially those in public relations.

Education Careers

Teachers in the early grades have the awesome task of teaching children how to read. And at every grade level, they have the opportunity to inspire children to become bookworms. You can't be an effective teacher without doing considerable reading to increase your knowledge. Classroom teachers read textbooks and accompanying teachers' manuals, professional journals, books, and magazines to enrich the curriculum for their students. University professors read and research to obtain their doctorates, then they continue reading and researching to publish scholarly works that will help them achieve tenure. In fact, the higher the teaching level, the more reading you will do as part of your job.

Research Careers

Never before has there been so much information that people want to access or put together in a meaningful way. And all this abundance of information can be found from ancient documents to Internet websites. Being a researcher often means reading all day on the job. Imagine yourself as a historian reading through the papers of past presidents, searching for the rationale behind important political decisions. Or you could be doing research at a pharmaceutical company to find information on effective herbal cures used in the eighteenth century. While jobs in research were once found primarily at universities, there are now abundant opportunities for research with the government, businesses, and think tanks.

Public-Sector Careers

Because the government is the largest single employer in North America, bookworms are likely to find many jobs that appeal to them in the public sector. The career options are endless, as the government employs people in just about every occupation the private sector does, as well as many found only in the public sector. At the federal and state or provincial levels, you could work for elected or appointed officials reading mail and handling constituent requests. On the local level, you could spend your time helping people search for property titles and more. Overall, your best chance for employment with the government is at the local level because this is where most of the jobs are.

Private-Sector Careers

In North America, the private sector is the area where the greatest number of jobs are. These jobs are scattered in thousands of businesses—large and small—throughout the United States and Canada. While most jobs in the private sector may require some reading, bookworms will want to gravitate toward those professions that require considerable reading. All doctors need to read to keep current in their profession, lawyers read a lot in preparing every case, and clergy members are required to do considerable reading to prepare their weekly sermons. Stockbrokers and corporate people also find themselves reading reports much of the day.

Even More Careers for Bookworms

Bookworms may want to go beyond looking for jobs in places where books are traditionally found: libraries, schools, and publishing companies. Bookworms may be perfect for jobs as translators, storytellers, genealogy researchers, and news clippers for individuals and companies. Every year, more possibilities emerge. However, it does take some investigation to discover these jobs. Then, of course, there is another ideal job for a true bookworm—being an author and writing books.

Job Qualifications

Bookworms speak frequently and eloquently about their love for books. They consider books not only as prized possessions but also as true friends. However, a love of books and reading is not sufficient qualification for many jobs that require a significant amount of reading. Education really counts. In many cases, having a bachelor's degree isn't even enough. Quite often a master's degree is a prerequisite for being considered for a position. And there are many jobs for bookworms where holding double master's degrees or a doctorate would be helpful. Fortunately, bookworms tend to want to study and receive as much education as possible. In preparing for a career, bookworms also need to realize that most reading jobs now require sophisticated computer skills.

How to Find the Perfect Job

As you read the personal career stories of bookworms in each chapter, pay special attention to how they got their jobs. You will discover that many of them found their jobs through networking. Even when you are searching for your first job, networking can be an effective job-search tool. Talk to college teachers in the field where you are searching for a job. Tell friends and family members that you are looking for a job. Ask them if they have any contacts who might be able to help you in your search. Besides newspaper ads and online job websites, visit the websites of associations in the field in which you are searching. Be sure to create an effective resume by reading printed and online materials and learn how to write a cover letter that will sell you to potential employers. And once you get a job interview, learn all you can about the organization. Have family and friends ask you potential interview questions to help you practice your responses. There is considerable advice in both printed materials and online websites to help you ace job interviews.

For Further Reading

John Adams demonstrated how well he knew what it was like to be a bookworm when he stated, "I read my eyes out and can't read half enough. . . . The more one reads the more one sees we have to read." Bookworms should become familiar with books like these in searching for the perfect job:

Bennett, Scott. *The Elements of Resume Style: Essential Rules and Eye-Opening Advice for Writing Resumes and Cover Letters That Work.* New York: AMACOM Books, 2005.

Dikel, Margaret Riley, and Frances E. Roehm. *Guide to Internet Job Searching 2008–2009.* New York: McGraw-Hill, 2008.

Enelow, Wendy S., and Louise Kursmark. *Cover Letter Magic: Trade Secrets of Professional Resume Writers.* Indianapolis, IN: JIST Works, 2006.

Oliver, Vicky. *301 Smart Answers to Tough Interview Questions.* Naperville, IL: Sourcebooks, Inc., 2005.

Powers, Paul. *Winning Job Interviews.* Franklin Lakes, NJ: Career Press, 2004.

United States Department of Labor. *The Big Book of Jobs 2007–2008.* New York: McGraw-Hill, 2006.

United States Department of Labor. *Occupational Outlook Handbook.* Indianapolis, IN: JIST Works, annual.

CHAPTER TWO

Library Careers

Connecting People with Everything in Print

onsider joining the close to five hundred thousand librarians and library workers in North America who have found one of the most perfect workplaces for bookworms—the library. No other career lets you spend your workday hanging out with stacks of books. While libraries have changed since your parents were kids, books still remain a librarian's major business even though libraries now house the most advanced media, including virtual libraries, the Internet, CD-ROM, and remote access to a wide range of resources. As a bookworm, there's another great advantage to working in a library: your coworkers as well as many library patrons are likely to be bookworms who share your passion for books and will be eager to talk to you about what they have read and want to read. Plus, there is the wonderful opportunity to hook children on books and help them learn the joy of being bookworms.

If you decide to work in a library, you will be in good company. Aristotle is probably the first well-known librarian. He gathered a collection of books for his school in Athens, founded in 347 B.C. Two famous colonial figures, Benjamin Franklin and Thomas Jefferson, were also librarians. Pinchpenny Franklin started a subscription library, limiting circulation to subscribers who paid a yearly fee. Not only did Jefferson catalog and classify materials for the University of Virginia library, his own personal library had ten thousand books. After the first Library of Congress burned, Jefferson's collection became the nucleus of the new library.

Being a librarian can lead to other careers. Pope Pius XI updated and reorganized the Vatican Library before he became pope. The Brothers Grimm, who wrote so many fairy tales, were librarians, too. Familiar modern figures who were librarians include J. Edgar Hoover, who worked at the Library of Congress while completing his law degree, and Mao Tse-tung, who was a library assistant at the Beijing University library. Mao carried periodicals to readers' tables and earned the same salary as an unskilled laborer. First Lady Laura Bush was a librarian, and, for a short time in recent years, an American astronaut even set up a small library on the Mir space station.

From four thousand years ago until today, the focus of the librarian's job is much the same. Librarians collect, organize, and make information available to people. What is new to the job is the important role technology plays in the work.

Where Librarians Work

When you choose to work as a librarian, it may not always be in a modern, comfortable, spacious environment. You may drive all day in a bookmobile, work next door to a laboratory with all its varied odors, or hand out books at a remote army base. All of this remarkable assortment of libraries in North America is usually divided into these four categories: public, school, academic, and special. But no matter whether a library is located at a zoo, in a law office, in a metropolitan area, or in a small rural community, the librarian is the person who provides the essential services. Hours on the job vary, with two out of ten librarians working part-time. School librarians usually have the same hours as teachers, except on the college level, where they may work on weekends. Most special librarians work normal business hours.

The Familiar Public Library

Bookworms are always well acquainted with the public libraries in their areas. And there is no shortage of libraries to visit. The

United States has approximately 16,500 central and branch public libraries, while Canada has more than 2,500. These libraries, which are usually supported locally, vary greatly in size. You can get lost in the huge New York Public Library with its seven million books or find yourself in a small one-room library within the Arctic Circle. Regardless of size or location, all public libraries require librarians to fulfill the same mission of serving the people who use them. This also means having at least a core of reference books for everyone in the community, plus sections with materials for children and adults. In some areas, libraries have sections to meet the special needs of a particular community. For example, the Detroit Public Library has a variety of materials on the history of the automobile, and the Toronto Public Library has a collection of pictures illustrating the history of Canada. Furthermore, most public libraries now have computers to give users access to library databases and the Internet.

School Libraries

The little old red schoolhouse typically did not have a library. However, in recent years, more and more schools in the United States have added libraries because teachers are asking their students to get information beyond what is in textbooks. Today, there are more than ninety-three thousand school libraries. The trend is just the opposite in Canada, where most public schools no longer have libraries. Those that do have libraries that are run by teacher-librarians and are open only for a limited number of hours.

The contents of school libraries tie closely to what is being taught at the schools. Obviously, high school libraries have a far wider range of materials than those in elementary, middle, or junior high schools. Because today's school libraries are also storehouses for films, filmstrips, recordings, videos, and graphic materials and provide access to all types of information through computers, they are now usually called library media centers or just media centers.

Academic Libraries

"Where are you going?" one college student asks another. Not surprisingly, the answer is often "to the library." Students go to the library to find information, to do research, and to study at the large tables or special study carrels. Not all academic libraries are the same. Community college libraries tend to cater to the needs of adult and vocational learners. College libraries vary greatly in size and scope. The library at Harvard University, with its close to sixteen million volumes, is the second largest in the United States. However, because of library networks and interlibrary loans, students at any university can obtain just about any book that they want. University libraries are usually the largest academic libraries. Many have very specialized collections on specific subjects. The gigantic University of California library system has collections devoted to subjects such as citrus fruits, California history, and oceanography. At a large university, you may find many separate libraries devoted to specific subjects located all over the campus.

Because of the knowledge boom that began in the 1950s and continues today, there has been a real increase in library building to store all this information. There has also been a fantastic increase in the use of computers in libraries to access all the information stored online throughout the world.

Special Libraries

Special is the key word to use in describing these libraries because they deal with specialized subjects, such as pharmacology, medicine, law, transportation, and religion. They have users who want special information, such as the federal requirements to be followed in removing asbestos or the best treatment for Parkinson's disease. Without these special libraries, people would find it impossible to keep up with the latest information in so many areas—especially in scientific fields. What follows is just a glimpse at some of the special libraries that exist, and all these libraries have jobs for librarians.

Government Libraries. The Library of Congress, the National Library of Medicine, and the Library of Agriculture are three government libraries in the United States that have developed such extensive collections that they are considered national libraries. In addition, the government operates an amazing number of libraries. Each branch of the armed services has technical, educational, and recreational libraries on a nationwide and worldwide basis. The navy even operates libraries on board ships. You will find libraries at Veterans Administration hospitals, the National Weather Service, the Patent and Trademark Office, the Environmental Protection Agency, and in virtually every department of the government. The states also operate their own libraries. The list of government libraries is almost endless. In Canada, Library and Archives is the national library, with the provinces also operating their own libraries.

Business Libraries. When employees at a firm need information, they can often find it in the company library. Special libraries can be found in businesses such as the following:

- banks
- accounting firms
- steel companies
- public utilities
- television stations
- aeronautics firms
- investment houses
- newspapers
- food-processing firms
- advertising agencies
- research institutes
- telephone companies

Science Libraries. The vast amount of scientific knowledge that is constantly being discovered, updated, and changed in scientific fields such as nutrition, marine biology, botany, physiology, biochemistry, zoology, and the health sciences necessitates libraries in a wide range of organizations, including:

- chemical companies
- cosmetics companies
- medical schools
- health centers
- hospitals
- petroleum refineries
- mining firms
- horticultural centers
- veterinary hospitals
- pharmaceutical firms

Would You Really Like to Be a Librarian?

You won't become a millionaire as a librarian, but you may have the opportunity to do a lot of reading. Being a bookworm, this should please you. However, you should realize that relatively few librarians have the luxury of sitting down on the job and reading a book from cover to cover. Of course, there are exceptions, such as the bibliographer at the national Library of Congress who spent forty years reading as he worked on a bibliography of snow, ice, and permafrost.

The librarian sitting behind a desk at your local library is doing far more than reading; he or she spends a lot of time answering questions and helping patrons. But the librarian also has the chance to see new books coming into the library, read reviews of books in an assigned area in order to find books to order, and assemble book lists. And in this age of technology, the librarian is now busy searching and helping patrons find information via the computer.

Do You Have the Necessary Qualifications?

Most library jobs require considerable versatility. However, there are certain personal competencies that most librarians share. Does the following list of personal competencies show that you have what it takes? Are you:

- an excellent communicator?
- a lover of books?
- a good problem solver?
- intellectually curious?
- conscientious?
- tactful and courteous?
- flexible?
- good with all kinds of people?
- service oriented?
- inquisitive?
- a decision maker?
- a team player?

In addition to the necessary personal qualifications, prospective librarians need to have certain professional competences, including meeting considerable educational requirements. Are you a person who:

- is willing to learn new technologies?
- uses current technology and tools?
- likes to do research?
- can manage a budget?
- can market library services?
- can build digital and print collections?
- can negotiate purchases?
- can meet information needs?

The Education of a Librarian

The amount of education needed depends upon the job that you want to hold. If you want to be a professional librarian in either the United States or Canada, the requirements are the same in order to work at most libraries: a master's degree in library science (M.L.S.) or library and information science (M.L.I.S.). This often takes at least a year beyond the bachelor's degree, but two-year programs are becoming common. A typical graduate program includes courses in the foundations of library and information science, including the history of books and printing, intellectual freedom and censorship, and the role of libraries and information in society. Other basic courses cover the selection and processing of materials, the organization of information, reference tools and strategies, and user services. Future librarians are also taught to use new resources brought about by advancing technology, such as online reference systems, Internet search methods, and automated circulation systems.

Although a number of colleges in the United States and Canada offer the M.L.S. degree, you will probably want to attend one that has a program accredited by the American Library Association. Admission to these programs isn't easy. Not only will you need good college grades (at least a B average), you may also need an acceptable score on the Graduate Record Examination. Librarians are quite an educated group. After obtaining an M.L.S., many take courses in continuing education throughout their careers. And librarians with specific goals often go on to earn certificates for advanced study programs, master's degrees in different fields, or even doctorates in library science.

Schooling Required for Professional Librarians

The educational requirements may vary depending on the career path you choose. Here is a brief discussion of several options.

Public Libraries. If you want a really high administrative post in a very large library, having a master's degree in library science may not be enough. You may find it helpful to have a Ph.D. in library science or an advanced business degree.

School Libraries. If you like working with school-age children and are seriously considering being a school librarian, check the department of education's certification requirements in the state or province where you want to work. It may be sufficient to have a bachelor's degree in education plus courses in library science. In some cases, you would need a master's degree in library science, perhaps with a library media specialization, or a master's in education with a specialty in school library media or education media.

Academic Libraries. Librarians wishing to teach library and information science or hold top administrative posts in college or university libraries will find it helpful to have doctorate degrees.

Special Libraries. Not only is a special librarian going to need an M.L.S., at least a bachelor's degree or possibly another master's degree is often required in the library's special subject area.

Schooling Required for Library Support Staff

Depending on where they work, the support staff of libraries have such titles as library technician, library clerk, library technical assistant, and library paraprofessional. These library employees need computer skills but certainly don't need the years of education beyond high school that professional librarians do. In fact, it is even possible to get a support staff position with just a high school diploma and on-the-job training. Many libraries, nevertheless, prefer support staff to have completed a two-year college program in library technology. Some even require a bachelor's degree.

Librarians Talk About Their Work

Librarians love to read and feel that they need to read all the time because so much new material is constantly being published. However, most librarians can't read as much as they want because they have so many other things to do on their jobs. Librarians do manage to keep current with literature in their specific areas by relying on professional journals, book lists, and reviews.

The basic tasks of librarians are largely the same whether they are working in a public, school, academic, or special library. To give you a better picture of what librarians do, some librarians describe their work on the following pages.

Library Assistant in a County Library

Katie Gallagher is a part-time library assistant who is studying for her M.L.I.S. degree. After graduation from college with a degree in theater, one of her early jobs was in a bookstore. This job showed Katie that she liked to be around books and led to her desire to become a librarian. After she started taking courses in library science, she looked around for a part-time job in a library. At first, she worked on the administrative side of a county library. When she saw a posting for a library clerk in the system, she applied for this job and got it.

At the library where she works, there is some crossover between what the assistants and librarians do. During her five-hour stint, Katie spends two to three hours on the desk or answering phone calls from patrons. The remaining time is usually spent processing new books or handling interlibrary loans. At times, she does some research to help patrons.

Katie realizes that working in a library will help her get a job as a librarian when she completes her degree. Right now, she thinks that she would like to find a job as a school librarian. Fortunately, her college also offers the courses and internships she would need to get this position.

Acquisitions Librarian at a Central Library

Kathy Barnard may have close to the perfect job for a bookworm. As a member of the department that selects books and other materials for a large public library, she chooses the books that the library will acquire for its branches. In one year, Kathy may recommend the purchase of a few thousand new books. This does not actually involve reading books on the job but rather reading reviews of books. Her job is challenging because she has to predict how popular a book will be with library patrons before it is even released. The easiest choices she makes are new books by well-known authors.

Kathy finds this job to be very satisfying because she has the opportunity to be so immersed in the world of books. Before acquiring this job, she worked as a reference librarian.

Reference Librarian in a Suburban Library

Because she is a confirmed bookworm, Stefanie van Ogtrop loved the idea of working in a library after graduating from college. Her first job in the world of books was as a clerk—an opening she saw in the local newspaper. After obtaining her M.L.S. degree, she became a young adult librarian and established programs appealing to this age group.

Today, Stefanie is branch manager of a suburban library. When she is not handling administrative responsibilities, she takes turns with two other librarians at the reference desk. She considers the job of reference librarian similar to being a detective. With six hundred to seven hundred patrons visiting the library every day, the questions vary enormously, from a schoolchild seeking information on a Texas governor of the 1800s to an adult looking for facts on global warming. Stefanie uses computer resources to answer many questions; however, she often finds it faster and easier to consult library books and other materials.

One of the best perks of Stefanie's job is having the chance to look at all the new books that arrive at the library. She always picks a few to browse. Her own need to read also widens her background and makes it so much easier to answer patrons' questions.

Library Administrator in a Large City

The higher you climb on the administrative ladder in a library, the shorter the amount of time you are likely to read on the job. Vivian Small remembers being assigned the delightful task of reading all of the award-winning Newbery and Caldecott books in one of her first jobs as a children's librarian. Plus, as both a children's librarian and a reference librarian, she spent considerable time reading reviews to select books to be added to the collections. Vivian even did some reading as the manager of a branch library, where she also served as a reference librarian. She was involved in the selection of new books and helping patrons find books that they would like. One of the most enjoyable aspects of this job was going to book warehouses and wandering up and down the aisles selecting books for her branch.

When Vivian became a supervising librarian of seven libraries in a large city, her contact with books and library patrons almost entirely vanished. Her job involved hiring and training library personnel, scheduling, budgeting, maintaining the facilities, and attending meetings. Nevertheless, this confirmed bookworm, who often got into trouble as a child because she was always reading, is still an avid reader who has a book in her hands whenever she can.

Research Librarian at a Business Magazine

Susann Rutledge is a confirmed bookworm. In fact, her earliest childhood memory centers on being in a library. As deputy manager in the research department at *BusinessWeek* magazine, she now gets paid to work in a library and read—an ideal situation for her. And she works with three researchers, one paraprofessional, and the library director, who also read on the job.

The librarians spend their days doing research for the magazine's reporters and editorial staff, who need information for their stories. As deputy manager, she is also responsible for keeping track of all requests that come into the office and making sure they are answered. The requests are prioritized, and the e-mail system is the primary method of tracking each request. In just a month, the researchers will answer as many as five hundred requests. While many queries cover different businesses and the stock market, plenty of others relate to politics, the entertainment industry, or advances in medicine. Most research is done online using databases.

Because there is so much information available, Susann and the other researchers have to evaluate very carefully what they have read in order to write a summary to fulfill each request. Some requests take just a few minutes to handle, while others may take hours. When research is so vital to a story that Susann becomes the reporter's right hand, she receives a byline credit. She has received credit for her work on several cover stories.

What kind of a background do you need to get a job like Susann's? She and the other librarians all have master's degrees in library and information science. How do you get these jobs that let you read? It can be very difficult as there is often very little turnover. This is especially true at her magazine. Susann had a summer internship in which she was able to demonstrate her solid research skills, and she was offered a full-time job after graduation. She recommends this job to anyone who loves to read and learn new things every day.

Manager of Library and Information Services at a Zoo

Suzanne Braun-McKee actually found her job as a zoo librarian through a newspaper ad that piqued her interest. While working at the zoo, she had the rare opportunity of building a brand-new library and developing a collection of books, journals, videos, and slides.

It was also her responsibility to continually expand the zoo's library to meet staff needs. In doing her job, she had to become an expert on materials ranging from orchids to rhinos.

To be successful in the special library field, Suzanne found it essential to use diverse reading skills. She spent a lot of time on the Web sifting through information for the zoo curators. Then, she had to use her critical-thinking skills and library background to determine what information was accurate and reliable. Much of her reading was of very technical materials, requiring her to analyze carefully what she had read.

As manager of the zoo library, Suzanne had to become a jack-of-all-trades as she juggled several duties that you might not expect a librarian to handle. She proofread all the publications of the zoo, wrote interpretive information signs, created handouts for general visitors, and sat on a lot of committees.

While Suzanne loves to read, her major reason for becoming a librarian was to disseminate knowledge. At the zoo, she was able to use what she read to help the staff and general public find out what they wanted to know.

Librarian at a Newspaper

Sylvia Halladay is currently a librarian at a major Midwest city newspaper. Before getting this job, she was a court librarian—working for judges. Along with two other full-time librarians and one part-time librarian, she has the task of entering into the newspaper's database the articles that reflect what was in the newspaper each day. Sylvia uses her computer to call up a page and go through it story by story. For some sections of the newspaper, she puts a subject header on every story and sends it to the database. In others, she only sends articles related to her state to the database. She also must check that each story's headline is in the database. If this hasn't been done automatically by the newspaper's computers, she enters the headline in the database and troubleshoots to learn why it didn't come automatically. The database that she and the other librarians are creating is used by the newspaper's reporters, paid databases, and the online paper for the public. She spends a little time doing research for reporters and handles other tasks, such as making a recipe database.

This is one job in which you actually read almost every minute of the day, so it is ideal for bookworms. It is also one in which computer skills are a must. Just a few years ago, the job of newspaper librarian was entirely different. Then the librarians would actually cut articles from the newspaper and file them under the appropriate headings.

Being a newspaper librarian is a small field. Some of the librarians at Sylvia's newspaper have M.L.S. degrees. And like most newspaper jobs, the librarians do shift work. Sylvia's shift is from 1 P.M. to 9:30 P.M. on Monday through Friday.

Library Director at a Law Office

A virtual library is not enough for lawyers; they still need law books. The large midwestern firm where Nikki Schofield works has more than ten thousand volumes. One part-time library assistant works with her to do loose-leaf filing. Nikki handles attorneys' requests, manages the budget, orders new material, catalogs books, recommends electronic services, and keeps track of circulation. One of her main tasks is overseeing the library's expenses.

Nikki's job is perfect for someone who loves to read because it is her major activity. Her job has changed in the past five years. Now, the research that she once did for lawyers is being handled by the paralegals and associates at the firm. This might not be true for librarians at other firms.

Nikki describes her job as challenging and never boring. She continues to hone her skills, focusing most of her attention on librarian conventions to learn new technology. When her workday is over, this bookworm just transfers her attention to reading books on the Civil War—her favorite avocation.

School Library Media Coordinator

What makes Joanne Fox's job satisfying as an elementary school librarian is the opportunity to teach children how to use the library and to acquaint them with the world of books. Every day, several classes come to the library. Joanne typically begins each half-hour session by reading and discussing an age-appropriate story with the children. Then she spends time on building their library skills before she helps them select books.

Besides working with the students, Joanne also helps the teachers select books to match their classroom curricula. Plus, time needs to be spent every day handling administrative tasks and directing the volunteer aides.

Considerable reading is involved in this job, as Joanne has to decide which books should be added to the library's collection of ten thousand volumes. Then, when the new books arrive, this bookworm always tries to read all the picture books and novels and as many other books as she can. As a result, she always has a stack of books by her bed at home.

In order to be a school librarian in her state, it was only necessary for Joanne to have a bachelor's degree. The principal chose her for this job because of her superior qualifications. She also had master's degrees in zoology and museum studies and had worked part-time in a public library.

The Good and Bad of Being a Librarian

Just like any other career, being a librarian has both positive and negative aspects. While this career may not let bookworms read as much as they like, it does allow them to spend time near their fondest possessions—books.

Good Things About Being a Librarian

- Part of the time in your job you are paid for doing what you love most—reading.
- You work with people who share your love of books.
- You have the opportunity to share your knowledge of books with library patrons.
- You can feel the reward of furthering other people's knowledge, whether they are esoteric researchers or third graders doing their first reports.

- You join a profession that demands you keep learning about what is happening in the world.
- You have a job that lets you use all your creativity and initiative in searching for hard-to-find materials.
- You can choose to be either a generalist or a specialist who concentrates on a particular field of interest.
- You can choose between working with people or working for the most part by yourself.

Things to Consider About Being a Librarian

- Considerable preparation is required for this career; librarians usually need to have master's degrees.
- Pay for librarians is not always equal to that of other professions that require the same amount of schooling.
- You may have to cope at times with unreasonable demands and discourteous behavior from library patrons.
- You may have to be able to stoop, lift, and stretch as you shelve or reach for books.
- You must be willing to use computers in searching for information at most libraries.
- You will not always work the typical nine-to-five day. Libraries are open in the evenings and on weekends.

Getting a Job as a Librarian

If you just want a clerical or a technical job in a library, you can usually find this type of work by contacting a local library, going online to job websites, or reading newspaper ads. However, a more concerted effort is generally needed to find a job as a librarian. Here are some ways to find these jobs.

American and Canadian Library Associations

One of the best ways to get solid information about a career as a librarian is by visiting the website of one of the national library associations. If you are interested in obtaining a library position in Canada, visit the Canadian Library Association (CLA) website at www.cla.ca. It also has helpful career and job information. The American Library Association (ALA) website at www.ala.org offers a career overview and information on salaries, job outlook, education and degrees, professional development, and employment opportunities. In an effort to help librarians and library workers find employment, ALA and its units list available positions in a variety of formats. Here are a number of resources available through the ALA website for job seekers:

- JobLIST: a service of American Libraries and C&RL News
- Library & Information Technology Association (LITA) job site: jobs in library information and technology
- ALA Placement Services: operates in conjunction with ALA Midwinter Meetings and the ALA Annual Conferences

Part-Time Jobs

You can begin paving the way for your first full-time job before you ever finish your education by working part-time in a library. Prior experience is always an added bonus on a resume. Furthermore, getting your foot in the door with a part-time job can lead to a full-time job after graduation.

Internships and Work-Study Programs

You should also look into other options for experience, such as internships and work-study programs. Besides extremely sought-after internships at the Library of Congress and the National Library of Medicine, many research, academic, and special libraries offer internships that can lead to future jobs.

Help on Campus

College placement services can really be helpful in finding a job. They post job listings, and many help with the writing of resumes and send your credentials to prospective employers. Don't overlook studying college bulletin boards and talking to faculty members, fellow students, and alumni when searching for a job.

Internet Resources

Be sure to visit www.libraryjobpostings.com. It links to all the various state and regional job Web pages. Another website to visit is www.lisjobs.com, which posts jobs for librarians and information professionals. Many general online job-search websites post information on library vacancies, too. Library associations and state library agency sites also list job openings.

Classified Ads

Most library journals have classified ad sections that list jobs. You can even advertise your own availability in some of these journals, listing your experience and education plus your preferences—job title, location, salary, and so forth.

Librarian Conventions and Conferences

Go to the conventions and conferences of library associations. Many have job placement programs. You can even send your credentials in before some conventions start.

Directory

The *American Library Directory* lists all kinds of libraries in a two-volume directory or online (www.americanlibrarydirectory .com). Its only weakness is that some school and special libraries don't return their forms so they aren't listed.

Federal Government Information

Don't overlook getting a job with the government. To work in many of the federal libraries in the United States, you must establish civil service eligibility and be placed on the Office of Personnel Management (OPM) register in the geographic area in which you wish to be considered. Other agencies, such as the Federal Bureau of Investigation, the Central Intelligence Agency, and

Library of Congress, have their own special procedures for hiring. Applicants should contact the agencies directly. In Canada, you can learn about hiring procedures and job opportunities by visiting the government's jobs website at http://jobs-emplois.gc.ca.

Making a Living as a Librarian

Your salary as a librarian will vary according to your qualifications and the type, size, and location of your workplace. Overall, the good news is that librarians' salaries are increasing. The annual American Library Association (ALA) survey in 2007 showed the median salary for ALA-accredited librarians with master's degrees was $57,809, with the median ALA M.L.S. salary being $53,000. Salaries ranged from $22,048 to $225,000. Salaries for librarians without M.L.S. degrees ranged from $10,712 to $143,700. For all positions, salaries are usually highest in the North Atlantic and West/Southwest regions and lowest in the Southeast. In Canada, the median salary for a librarian in a large city is more than CAN$50,000. You can get a better idea of what you might make as a librarian by studying the salaries listed in online ads for librarians and in professional journals.

What Else Can You Do with a Library Degree?

Just because you graduated from college with a librarian's degree is no reason you have to become a librarian. Librarians can use their specialized knowledge in many other satisfying careers requiring similar analytical, organizational, communication, and database skills. Look at this list of book-related and information-related careers many librarians are pursuing:

- researcher
- bookseller
- archivist

- editor
- information consultant
- indexer
- storyteller
- author
- abstractor
- information broker
- records manager
- database specialist
- systems analyst
- book reviewer
- historian
- information systems manager
- museum curator
- publisher's sales representative
- webmaster or Web developer

The Future Outlook for Librarians

Today, there is an explosion of knowledge both in printed and online material in every field that you can think of. Former American Library Association President John W. Berry has described current librarians as the human search engines we increasingly count on to help us sort through all this information.

Jobs for librarians in the United States will grow the fastest in the next decade for those working in nontraditional librarian jobs, including work as information brokers and for private corporations, nonprofit organizations, and consulting firms. While the number of librarians working in traditional settings is expected to grow more slowly than for all occupations through 2014, opportunities are expected to be very good because so many librarians are retiring and fewer people are entering the profession. In some cases in recent years, there have been more jobs than applicants. In Canada, the number of job seekers is likely to match the number of openings, with more openings occurring as librarians retire.

For Further Reading

The image of a librarian sitting behind a desk checking books in and out is decidedly not a description of today's librarians. Although this may still be part of the job, librarians have become information specialists adept at using computers to search for written material throughout the world. Learn more about career opportunities for librarians by reading the following career books:

Carvell, Linda P. *Career Opportunities in Library and Information Science.* New York: Ferguson Publishing Company, 2005.

Raddon, Rosemary, ed. *Your Career, Your Life: Career Management for the Information Professional.* Burlington, VT: Ashgate Publishing Company, 2004.

Shontz, Priscilla K., and Richard A. Murray, eds. *A Day in the Life: Career Options in Library and Information Science.* Portsmouth, NH: Libraries Unlimited, 2007.

For more specific information on careers in special libraries, visit the following websites:

Special Libraries Association: www.sla.org
American Association of Law Libraries: www.aallnet.org
Medical Library Association: www.mlanet.org

CHAPTER THREE

Book Publishing Careers

Bringing New Books to Everyone

Step into any of the new super-size bookstores and you will be able to view as many as two hundred thousand books. What is more amazing is that all the shelves in these bookstores could be full to overflowing with just the books published in North America each year. There is definitely no shortage of books for bookworms to read. And the exciting thing is that each book is likely to have passed through the hands of editors, proofreaders, designers, and printers before it ever reached readers' hands. Any one of these jobs is a great career choice for bookworms who wish to work closely with books every day.

These books are published by major commercial publishers, small commercial houses, university presses, nonprofit publishers, scholarly societies, and individuals publishing their own books. Each presents job opportunities for bookworms. In the United States there are large publishers such as McGraw-Hill, Random House, Simon & Schuster, John Wiley & Sons, HarperCollins, Pearson, Penguin, Houghton Mifflin, Hachette Book Group USA, and Macmillan. Many of these companies also have branches in Canada, where there are more than six hundred publishing houses of varying sizes. Jobs are definitely not limited to large publishers as there are more than three thousand medium-size publishers in North America, as well as more than eighty thousand small or self-publishing companies. If you decide to work for a major book publisher, you are likely to work in a large city. In the United States, these publishers are concentrated in New York City. However, you may find yourself in California, where there are more small publishers than in any other state.

A career in this industry can be just right for a confirmed bookworm because so many jobs in book publishing involve considerable reading. There are jobs that let you:

- read manuscripts all day and decide whether they will be published
- edit the author's writing to make it better
- sell books to bookstores and schools
- find typographical errors that a typesetter has made
- write your opinion of the books being published

A Glimpse into the Book Publishing Industry

Browse through a bookstore and you will find children's books, travel books, religious books, home-improvement books, cookbooks, romance novels, and an amazing number of other kinds of books. Most of these are called trade books, and they make up about one-third of all the books sold. Textbooks for students from kindergarten through college are the next largest category of books sold in North America. There is also a market for reference books, such as dictionaries, encyclopedias, and atlases, as well as for scholarly books put out by university presses. Some companies publish a wide variety of books on a broad range of subjects, while others only fill a particular niche.

The largest companies may employ thousands of people, while the smallest may only have two employees—the publisher and an assistant. You are more likely to have a specific job, such as copyeditor or proofreader, at a larger firm; at a smaller firm, you could wear several hats at once.

You may find it helpful to know what the usual editorial organization chart looks like in a large publishing company:

- Executive Editor
- Editor—Managing or Acquisitions
- Associate Editor
- Assistant Editor
- Editorial Assistant

Naturally, this chart will look slightly different at each publishing house. Copyeditors can be part of the above hierarchy as assistant or associate editors; however, in large houses they are usually found in a separate department.

Where to Start

The starting point for most careers in the publishing industry is at the bottom of the editorial ladder. After advancing to the position of assistant editor, many elect to move to other companies. For some the move is to a larger or smaller publishing house, while others elect to move a house that publishes in one area, such as education, romance novels, or children's books.

Starting as an Editorial Assistant

You'll never get bored starting in the publishing industry as an editorial assistant because of the large variety of tasks you will be required to do. There will be plenty of tedious jobs, such as word processing, filing, verifying facts, and returning unacceptable manuscripts. The good news is that you will probably be able to do quite a bit of reading on the job as soon as you know how the publishing house works.

Much of your reading will center on going through the "slush" pile, which is the accumulation of unsolicited manuscripts that drown most publishers. You will be evaluating the potential of each manuscript. You won't be able to select manuscripts for consideration just because you like them; they will have to fit with what the publishing house prints. For example, a Christian publishing house will not be looking for steamy romance stories.

Sometimes getting an entry-level job can be based upon who you know. A burned-out schoolteacher found a job as a junior editor at a children's publishing house because she knew someone who worked there. This job led to her becoming a children's book editor. As an editorial assistant, called "junior editor" at her company, her work was not glamorous. She typed, filed, researched, and learned to edit with the help of an editor. Gradually, she was given books to edit.

Steps on the Editorial Ladder

After one or two years as an editorial assistant, you will probably begin to move up the editorial ladder. The irony is that the higher you climb, the less time you will be able to devote to reading because so many administrative tasks intervene. Many senior editors find that their job-related reading has become their homework. They do it while they commute, in the evening, on weekends, and on holidays.

Assistant Editor—a Reader's Job

Up one notch from an editorial assistant, the assistant editor at most publishing houses primarily does copyediting and proofreading. At this level, bookworms should be in heaven because there is so much reading to do. Be warned, though, that some assistant editors are weaned away from reading to become more involved with the editorial production of books. This can mean working with the art department or designers on page layout and illustrations.

Copyeditor

In some publishing houses, the assistant editor is essentially a copyeditor. Copyeditors usually get manuscripts from editors who have worked on the content and organization but leave it to the copyeditor to fix what is still wrong. No two copyeditors have exactly the same job. At some houses, they may do considerable rewriting, while at others they only mark typographical errors. In either case, copyeditors are responsible for checking spelling, grammar, and punctuation. They look for inconsistencies in copy, such as first boarding a plane and later disembarking from a ship (rather than the plane). They also look for inconsistencies in style, such as whether to spell out numbers or abbreviate street names. They may be required to check for factual accuracy or confirm addresses or websites. They find and eliminate repetitions. They read an entire manuscript paragraph by paragraph, line by line, and word by word. Many copyeditors now use computers, but some still prefer to use good old-fashioned pencils and write directly on the manuscripts.

A manuscript is always read more than once because copyediting also involves keeping track of the plot and making sure that events fall into the correct slots on a time line. Often the first reading is quick to get the overall idea. The next reading involves marking errors. Corrections are made, then after a final rereading, the manuscript goes back to the author. The author may also make changes, which are copyedited in another reading. The manuscript is checked again when it comes back from the typesetter and every time any changes are made in the copy.

Proofreader

Do you have the eyes of an eagle? Are you good at finding typographical errors on the printed page? Do you have the ability to scrutinize manuscripts closely? Are you a good speller? Even if you answer yes to the above questions, you will need to be able to prove your proofreading skills by taking a test that includes spelling and grammar before you are hired.

Proofreading involves checking that copy from the printer exactly matches the manuscript. To proofreaders, finding inconsistencies is almost like a game. Training is required for this job. Many proofreaders have academic training; more have probably learned on the job. Although some proofreaders work in-house, sometimes with the job title of assistant editor, many publishing houses send proofreading jobs to freelancers.

Associate Editor—a Varied Position

After working for a few years as an assistant editor, the next step at many companies is associate editor. It's a good promotion for a reader because it means less clerical work but still involves considerable reading. At the same time, of course, the responsibilities increase. This usually means more contact with authors, especially because you have the authority to make more changes in manuscripts. You make rewrite suggestions for cuts and additions and have far more leverage in how a book is edited. In addition, you may begin to become involved in the acquisition of new books.

Editor—Managing or Acquisitions

What an editor does varies greatly from company to company. Some publishing houses have separate positions for managing and acquisitions editors. At other houses, an editor is both a managing and an acquisitions editor. How much editors read truly depends on what their responsibilities are. Some still do quite a lot of reading at their offices, while others spend most of the time working on the business side of publishing.

Managing Editor. These editors are in charge of day-to-day operations. They see that schedules are maintained and supervise junior editors. Managing editors typically oversee the work of the copyeditors, proofreaders, and, in many cases, the designers and illustrators, who are responsible for the way books look.

Acquisitions Editor. These are the editors who have lunches with authors, go to book signings, and attend book fairs. They have the task of bringing in and signing up new books and authors and working with literary agents. They are also supposed to come up with new book ideas.

Executive Editor

At the top of the editorial ladder is the executive editor who has almost always climbed the ladder rung by rung to reach this position. Executive editor jobs are typically found at large publishing houses where they oversee the assistant and associate editors.

Executive editors often direct the overall planning and editorial content of the company's publications. They spend time coordinating art, text, prepress, and manufacturing to ensure proper control over production schedules, implementation of technology, quality, and cost. In addition, they may develop long-range plans and monitor developments in the publishing industry to assess all of the far-reaching implications of trends for their companies.

This job requires great involvement in the business side of publishing books. The executive editor makes major decisions on budgeting, scheduling, acquisitions, and marketing strategies. Time is also spent on developing ideas for new books and monitoring the progress of projects. Only a very limited amount of time is spent reading and editing manuscripts.

Publisher or President

At many publishing houses, there is a publisher or president at the top directing the entire operation. Although publishers tend to be bookworms, this is not a hands-on manuscript job. It involves supervising every department of the company. This job involves a lot of reading, but it is in the form of memos, financial statements, and professional journals.

Book Publishers Talk About Their Work

Read on for several views of the world of book publishing; five professionals share the paths they followed into their rewarding careers.

Assistant Editor—Romances

Harlequin Enterprises, which publishes more than 115 romance books each month, is Canada's most successful publisher. The entry-level position on the editorial side at Harlequin is assistant editor. To obtain this position, you have to demonstrate the ability to read a book and know if it meets the company's standards, fix a story so it flows, critique a plot, edit text, and write cover copy. Most successful applicants have degrees in English.

Assistant editors at Harlequin begin working under senior editors, who supervise the training. One thing they have to learn is how to write revision letters, which explain the changes editors think would improve an author's manuscript. Assistant editors read senior editors' revision letters as part of acquiring this skill. They also read submissions from the "slush" pile to find possible new acquisitions.

Each assistant editor is assigned a stable of authors who regularly write Harlequin books. He or she edits these books and begins to find his or her own repeat authors from the slush pile.

Editor at a Trade Book Company

The editorial assistant who was described earlier worked her way up the ladder to become an editor of children's books. In this job, she wears the hats of both a managing and an acquisitions editor.

Every fourth week, she becomes an acquisitions editor and goes through as many as seventy-five books in a week. Not all of the seventy-five books are read cover to cover. However, after careful scanning and skimming, each book is placed in a pile indicating its future, such as whether it will be sent on to the acquisitions editor or returned to the author. This editor clearly knows what she likes and what her company is looking for. She discusses her acquisition choices with other editors. If the majority approves a book, it is sent to the marketing department for a yes or no vote. While wearing the hat of managing editor, this editor oversees the production of as many as twenty books in a year. Not only does she decide on text changes, she also acts as a copyeditor, which is something not all editors do.

In describing the pluses and minuses of her job, this editor points out that the job is not dull or routine. Because the subject matter varies greatly, the opportunity to learn something new is always there. The one negative to her job is the tension she feels when she falls behind on her schedule.

President of Free Spirit Publishing

Not all publishing companies are large. In the early days of Free Spirit Publishing, which started in 1983, Judy Galbraith was author, editor, business manager, and office manager. Today, the company has a staff of thirty-four full-time employees, including a director of finance and operations, a publishing director, an education sales director, an art director, and several editors, including one editorial assistant, one senior editor, and three editors. Other employees handle a variety of jobs, from order processing and shipping to customer assistance and editorial research.

Not all publishers rise through the editorial ranks to achieve their positions. Judy Galbraith was a teacher who started Free Spirit Publishing after purchasing the publishing rights to her first book, which had been published by another publisher. The company has grown steadily and currently has two hundred titles in print. Judy loves to read but is compelled to devote her office hours to the publishing business. However, at home, after work, and on weekends and airplane trips, she spends hours reading trade publications and manuscripts.

The Career Path of an Editor at a Major Publishing House

Amy White is a confirmed bookworm with undergraduate and master's degrees in English—a very common major for those working in the publishing industry. Applying for a job she saw in a newspaper ad led to her first position in publishing as an associate acquisitions editor at a small publishing house. Amy describes this as a fun job because she got to read and loved to research. She was given projects to do such as finding authors for coffee table books, gift books, and quote books. Then she oversaw the contracts with the authors, the development of the artwork, and the creation of the manuscripts. She also checked that each author was meeting the publisher's schedule and guidelines. She learned how to do her job by working with an acquisitions editor who was her go-to person when she had questions. Before Amy left this publisher, she was promoted to acquisitions editor overseeing other associate editors.

For her next job, Amy moved to a medium-size publishing house as acquisitions editor. While she was still looking for authors, her position expanded to obtaining reviews for recently completed books. Then her next career move was to a major publishing house where she read manuscripts sent in by agents and independent writers. She also continued researching and finding authors for projects appropriate to her assigned publishing area.

A move to a small education publishing house gave Amy the opportunity to advance up the career ladder and become an editor. In this job, she had to develop new project ideas as well as find authors for them. She was also directly involved in the editing, copyediting, and proofreading of these projects. Amy heard about this job through networking with another editor she had met at the major publishing house.

Today, Amy is back at the major publishing house where she had worked as acquisitions editor. She learned about this job through an editor who formerly worked at the small education publishing house. She now has a contract as an editor to complete an education project. Hiring editors to do specific projects is becoming quite common in the publishing industry. If there are more projects on the horizon at this house when she completes her current contract, she is likely to be hired on a full-time basis. Amy spends most of her day reading manuscripts as she edits content.

Career Advice. Amy wants to stress the importance of networking in obtaining editorial jobs in the publishing industry. It has helped her go far in her career.

The Path to Owning Your Own Editorial Firm

As a child, Betsy Lancefield Lane loved the way a good book read. She particularly loved the rhymes of Dr. Seuss. Even then, she wanted to make things sound pretty—the reason she ultimately became an editor. First, however, she had a career as a teacher, which she interrupted to earn a graduate degree in education and anthropology. Editing, however, was truly in her blood, as she was always editing papers for fellow students in graduate school. So Betsy went to Chicago to pursue a career in publishing. At the time, she had no idea that the editorial side of publishing was so competitive. Through networking, she learned of jobs and soon had two companies wooing her. She took a job with a small house and began her career as an assistant editor for two of its divisions—career books and business books. Betsy was asked to do a lot in this job, which helped her learn how the book industry works. In fact, she was truly a girl Friday. She would check page proofs, send out projects to freelancers and check that they were returned on time, work with the production manager to see all books were on schedule, and even make sure that the pages in a book were in the right order and the table of contents listed the chapters correctly. Advancement for Betsy was rapid in this company. Within six months, she became an associate editor and then the editor in charge of career books when that editor left.

After several years as editor, Betsy reached the top of the editorial ladder by becoming the editorial director at a midsize company that produced educational books and games. Here, she was in charge of all the editors, managing the editorial division's backlist and frontlist titles and, most importantly, having the vision for how best to develop the editorial product line.

Today, Betsy has formed her own business—Lane Editorial. It is increasingly popular for editors to do this as publishers are now outsourcing much of their editorial work. She loves the flexibility of being her own boss and has found no difficulty in finding work because of all of her previous networking with other editors. She now spends her days writing and editing and handling the business side of her company.

Career Advice. Betsy started out thinking it was best to work for a large publisher. Now, she believes that both larger and smaller companies have much to offer.

Indexing—a Career Within the Publishing Industry

Indexing is truly a great job for bookworms because a love of books is a necessity in this career. Plus, it also gives you the opportunity to do freelance work in the publishing industry because few companies have full-time indexers on staff. Furthermore, some publishing houses leave indexing up to authors, who, in turn, often look for freelance indexers to do this work.

In creating an index, an indexer makes an alphabetical list of a book's contents and lists page numbers where each item is discussed. Here is a job where a bookworm is being paid to read a book. Although books on every subject from podiatry to forestry are indexed, you will need some experience in a subject to index a book. Most indexers have advanced degrees and specialize in certain subjects. The job also requires organizational skills and the ability to determine what is important in a book. Computer skills are a must because indexing has gone high tech. Doing indexes on three-by-five cards is a thing of the past. In addition, indexers must be able to function well under pressure. Indexing is always a rush job because indexers are the last in line to get copy—the index is only begun when the final page layout has been completed. They must also be willing to work independently.

Professional Organizations for Indexers

The indexing field is a small one. Many indexers in the United States belong to the American Society for Indexing (ASI). Through ASI membership, indexers get a subscription to *Key Words: The Bulletin of the American Society for Indexing*, a discounted optional subscription to *The Indexer: The International Journal of Indexing*, and discounts on ASI conferences and workshops and other ASI publications. Members also have access to a health insurance program. Furthermore, membership in this organization gives indexers the opportunity to talk with others in their profession at local organizations of the society. Information can be obtained by visiting its website at www.asindexing.org.

Members of the Indexing Society of Canada (ISC) receive the organization's journal and bulletin, can attend annual conferences, and may participate in the e-mail forum. They also have the opportunity to be listed in the ISC's annual register of indexers. You can learn more about this organization by visiting its website at www.indexers.ca.

Acquiring Indexing Skills

You need some training to become an indexer. A publisher is going to expect you to have specific knowledge about indexing. Some indexing courses can be found at colleges that have schools of library or information science. The U.S. Department of Agriculture (USDA) offers two correspondence courses (Basic Indexing and Applied Indexing). For further information about these courses, contact:

USDA Customer Service Center
600 Maryland Avenue SW, Suite 120
Washington, DC 20024
www.grad.usda.gov

Courses are also offered through professional associations. The American Society for Indexing offers a distance-learning course for its members and also has information about other training courses on its website. The Indexing Society of Canada also provides course information on its website.

Working as an Indexer

You can make a living as a freelance indexer. Although what you are paid will vary from area to area, you will earn more if you are very fast or can handle very complicated material. The most common method of billing is charging for each indexable page, typically $3 to $6 per page in the United States and CAN$3 to CAN$7 in Canada. You can also be paid per entry or a flat fee for the job. You get indexing jobs through contacts with editors and other indexers and by sending resumes to publishers. Currently, the best opportunities lie in indexing educational, computer, business, science, and medical materials. In addition, new employment opportunities for indexers are available making indexes of online materials and CD-ROMs.

An Indexer at World Book

David Pofelski feels lucky to work at a company as an indexer. There are not many of these jobs. After college, he had no idea what he would like to do, except he felt publishing was an intriguing area. He found a job at Encyclopaedia Britannica as an indexer and has remained in this field throughout most of his career. He spent nine years at home working as a freelancer, doing his indexing on index cards before purchasing a computer. David has been at World Book since 1988. His indexing work continues to involve printed materials, but he also performs other editorial tasks related to online materials.

Indexing has become far more mechanized since the switch away from index cards to computers in the 1970s and 1980s. Indexers no longer have to worry so much about clerical details and are free to concentrate on the quality of what they produce. The advent of the computer has also cut the number of indexers.

David enjoys his job because he likes to read and especially likes reading a variety of materials and learning so much about different subjects. He approaches indexing as a craft and tries to do the best possible job on each index. The job has some negative aspects. He spends his entire day looking at a terminal, and there is considerable clerical work keying words in and checking for accuracy. He also works under tremendous pressure to get jobs done quickly.

A Freelance Indexer

For thirty years, Susan Holbert has been a freelance indexer. She believes that it is a perfect job for those who want to work at home and actually make money. It is also the ideal job for Susan, who is physically unable to work in an office. For years, she even had to do her indexing work lying down. Susan has indexed books ranging from a programming textbook to the autobiography of First Lady Rosalynn Carter, and she has worked for the United States and Massachusetts governments, as well as for numerous technology and business firms.

Susan is a true indexing expert. Besides her work as an indexer, she has created two very popular indexing seminars (one for freelancers and one for technical writers), given indexing workshops and presentations, and helped design and market an indexing software program, wINDEX. Visit www.abbington.com/holbert to learn more about this indexer, to take her "Is Indexing for You?" quiz, and to learn more about how to become an indexer.

Literary Agent—Another Publishing Profession

Just because an author writes a book doesn't mean you'll ever be able to find that book on a library shelf. It isn't easy for an author to get a book published, especially because many publishing companies won't even look at a manuscript unless a literary agent submits it. In North America, there are more than five hundred literary agencies. Whether an agency is run by one person or has hundreds of employees, the dream they all share is to find the next bestseller.

Literary agents represent authors to potential publishers, and they also act as negotiators between the two. Today, due to time and budget restraints, more publishers are relying on literary agents to produce new authors and materials.

Literary agents' days are never routine. They always buzz with activity. A typical day may include working with authors, editors, lawyers, and accountants. Agents may suggest changes to an author that will make a book more marketable, mediate a conflict between an author and an editor, as well as boost the flagging spirits of yet another author. They may try to convince an editor that an author in the agency's stable has just written a novel that will become a classic—or at least will sell more than ten thousand copies. The agents may wheel and deal with lawyers to get the best contract for a first-time author. They may check recent sales figures with accountants. More than likely, they will also suffer rejection from time to time. Some books that they absolutely love will never be sold to a publisher. Others may take years to sell. Rejection, even frequent rejection, is an accepted part of a literary agent's job.

Between all the paperwork and the never-ending phone calls, literary agents do not have a lot of time for reading during office hours. Yet reading is an important part of a literary agent's work; it is the only way to discover books to sell to editors. So reading time must be snatched whenever possible at the office, but most of it is done after hours.

You don't just set up shop as a literary agent. Most literary agents are former editors who have an eye for manuscripts that will sell. They can read the first thirty pages of a manuscript or the proposal for a book and know right away whether or not it has possibilities. Besides being able to recognize a saleable manuscript, a literary agent is really a jack-of-all-trades who has the ability to:

- handle people effectively
- shape an author's career
- know where different manuscripts can be sold
- negotiate contracts
- help authors edit their manuscripts

Bookworms can enjoy even an entry-level position as an assistant in a literary agency. The job involves many of the same duties as an editorial assistant. However, because many of the agencies are small, an assistant at an agency does more reading than in a large publishing house. The job could include reading manuscripts and writing reviews; typing and filing correspondence to authors and publishers; and scheduling meetings among authors, agents, and publishers. Some assistants become full-fledged agents or editors at publishing firms, while a few start their own agencies.

Book Reviewer

Imagine getting a free copy of a book and then being paid to read it. That's what happens when you are a book reviewer. Because the job is so appealing, there are a great number of book reviewers. Unfortunately, only a few of them are working on salary at this job. For that reason, freelancers usually write book reviews.

Book reviewers are normally paid for each review. How much you receive for a review depends on the size of the newspaper or magazine, the length and complexity of the review, and, occasionally, on your reputation as a reviewer. You could receive nothing except a new book or as much as $500. By selling the same review to different markets in geographically separated areas or in shorter or longer versions, it is possible to increase your income. You might be able to make as much as $1,000 for a single review.

To become a book reviewer, you need to be more than an avid reader; you also must have writing ability. You can learn how to be an expert book reviewer by studying book reviews that others have written and by taking courses. Just working in the publishing industry can also give you some of the experience you need.

Reading a book is the easiest part of being a book reviewer. The hardest is finding someone who wants you to write a review. Dave Wood, former book editor of the *Minneapolis Star Tribune*, had the names of 250 book reviewers in his file. During a typical year, fewer than half of these reviewers would actually write reviews for the newspaper. Only fifty to sixty of them were asked frequently to write reviews.

The road to being one of the lucky people chosen to write a review is a rough one. What you have to do is send a resume and samples of your work to newspapers and magazines. This often accomplishes nothing more than getting your name in a Rolodex file. You can also send unsolicited reviews. If an editor is looking for the book you reviewed, you may be on your way to becoming paid for reviewing books.

Book reviewers with some experience, even if it is for a small newspaper or magazine, can join the National Book Critics Circle. The organization publishes a newsletter and offers regional and national seminars that provide helpful information for book reviewers. You can join the National Book Critics Circle if you write a minimum of three book reviews a year and pay a fee. For information, visit the website at www.bookcritics.org. On this site, you will find very helpful tips for breaking into and staying in this profession.

Reviewing Books for a Magazine

One of the first places in which books are reviewed is *Publishers Weekly*. Valiska Gregory reviews four to six children's books each month for this magazine. Usually, the books are so new that she is reading from color proofs that are not even bound together.

When she reviews a children's book, Valiska tries to assess the author's purpose from the text and illustrations. She always reads a book more than once. She doesn't follow any particular format in writing her reviews, but she does try to indicate what the book is about as well as assess the book's literary and artistic merit. She often compares a book to similar ones.

Valiska, who is an author and poet as well as a freelance book reviewer, obtained her reviewing job through personal contacts. While attending a publishing course, she met a woman who became an editor of *Publishers Weekly*.

Reviewing Books for a Newspaper

Working in the library at a newspaper gave Betsy Caulfield the opportunity to meet the book editor and led to her becoming a freelance book reviewer. As a dedicated bookworm, Betsy always read book reviews. She got the idea of becoming a reviewer because she frequently disagreed with reviewers of books that she had read and wanted to share her opinion with others. She now reviews about one book each month after reading the entire book to get its essence.

Book Club Selector

Book clubs are not as popular as they once were since the advent of online bookstores. Nevertheless, many devoted bookworms still purchase their books from book clubs. Besides the well-known Book-of-the-Month Club and Doubleday Book Club that offer books in both the United States and Canada, there are specific clubs that cater to interests ranging from cooking, astronomy, and religion to photography, farming, and ecology. Children's books are offered through many of these clubs as well as separate children's clubs. Each club typically offers the opportunity to purchase new selections along with backlist titles.

Like the climber who reaches the top of Mount Everest, a bookworm who becomes a selector for a book club has reached the summit of his or her dreams. This job involves reading books and then deciding which should be offered to members. At some clubs, all the selectors are in-house editors reading literally from nine to five. At other houses, the editors do most of their reading at home while attending to marketing and administrative chores on the job. Most houses also use freelance selectors, who do a first reading and are typically paid between $50 and $100 per manuscript.

Bookworms who become selectors usually have bachelor's degrees behind their names. Their degrees don't have to be in English, but they usually are in some area of liberal arts. It is possible to get a job as a selector right after graduating from college. However, many get this job after working as administrative assistants, copyeditors, or at some other job in publishing. Don't bother applying for this job unless you are a speed reader. You should be able to read a thousand pages in twelve to fifteen hours.

Working as a Book Selector

"Sometimes, the pages just turned themselves," according to Jaye Isler, who was an editorial assistant at a major book club. At other times, she didn't even complete a book because she could determine early on that it wasn't right for the book club's members. Jaye, like other selectors, is a confirmed book lover. She confesses that she would far rather meet an author than a Hollywood star.

Jaye's job as an editorial assistant was a busy one with long hours. She didn't usually read manuscripts at the office but was involved in such things as making sure that books that were to be listed in the club's magazine were in stock and that there were pictures of these books. She also checked that the copy describing the books was accurate. At any given time, she was working on book information that would go in any one of eight selection magazines. In addition, she spent considerable time in meetings and negotiating with publishers to obtain the rights to a book.

Outside the office, Jaye read for approximately ten hours a week. During that time, she would read two or three books to determine whether the club should offer them to its members. When selectors begin working at Jaye's book club, they learn how to do the job by reading book evaluations that experienced selectors have made. At first, their evaluations are checked to make sure they understand what the club is looking for. "The longer one selects books for a club," Jaye says, "the easier it becomes to tell which books will satisfy the club members." Today, Jaye spends much of her time writing; however, she still spends some time reading and making selections for the book club.

Bookstore Owner

To a bookworm, owning an independent bookstore must seem like the best of all possible worlds. You can choose the books that you want for the store and consider new books before they are even bound. Nevertheless, there are black clouds in this business. The advent of Internet and chain bookstores has led to the closing of many independent stores, and the profit margin is typically a mere 2 percent. Still, many wonderful independent bookstores remain, to the delight of bookworms who love the ambiance and special services offered by these stores.

Owner of a Children's Bookstore

Before Shirley Mullin became a bookstore owner, she was a teacher. Now she owns her own bookstore in the Midwest called Kids Ink. Bookstore owners get to do a lot of job-related reading, and Shirley sees most new children's books from six to nine months before they are published. When she first sees a book, she is usually not looking at the finished copy but at prepublication galleys for the book. She reads all of the children's picture books herself but doesn't have time to read all of the other books, so she farms some of them out to her staff. Shirley often reads reviews, which usually come out after she has read the galleys for new books. By reading the reviews, she can see if she has missed any promising new books or if she wishes to reexamine any books that she has read. Shirley is also helped in her selection process by knowledgeable publishing company representatives.

Retail Bookstore Worker

Along with libraries, bookstores seem the perfect habitat for bookworms. And there is a wide choice of workplaces, ranging from small, specialized shops to superstores. The managers of these stores are actively searching for bookworms who really know books—from popular bestsellers to less-well-known offerings from small publishing houses. In a bookstore, surrounded by books, a bookworm may not have too much opportunity to read on the job. However, bookstore employees are encouraged to read book reviews and books so that they can help customers find the books they want. At many stores, the owners and managers also want employee input on what books should be added to a store's stock. An added dividend is that bookstore employees can often purchase books for a discounted price.

More Jobs Associated with Books

The more you learn about all the steps involved in bringing a book from author to reader, the more you'll know about the great variety of jobs that will actually let you read books. Taking an entry-level job or an internship are two ways many bookworms have become acquainted with interesting jobs like the following.

Designing Books

Someone has to decide just what a finished book is going to look like so it will appeal to readers. All the artwork, the headings, and the arrangement of the material on the pages have to be related to what is said on the pages. Each book needs a design theme. A job working in this area can tie your interest in books with an artistic background.

Illustrating Books

Illustrations are an important part of many books and must tie closely to the text. In order to do this successfully, the illustrator needs to read the manuscript carefully. Children's books and textbooks are usually full of illustrations. At times, illustrating is done in-house, but more often freelance illustrators do it.

Selling Books

For a bookworm, it's a lot more enjoyable to sell books than to sell aluminum siding or automobiles. Working as a sales representative for a publisher or distributor not only gives you the chance to read many of the books that you are trying to sell, you also get to talk about them to bookstore owners, buyers for chains, and librarians.

If you are selling textbooks, you will talk to both teachers and selection committees. No matter where you are selling books, your commission will be based on how well you know the product—books. Being a sales representative is a great career for a bookworm because the more you read, the more you earn, and you get the added benefit of traveling.

In this position, everyone learns on the job. The better you sell, the better your territory will be. Success in sales can also lead to management job offers in the home office. Some sales representatives even branch off on their own and become independent sales representatives.

More Career Possibilities

Even more career opportunities exist in book publishing for bookworms. You won't just find jobs with publishers. Book jobbers and distributors, direct- and subscription-mail sales organizations, and bookstore chains are other areas where bookworms can find jobs that let them be close to books in some way. You may also want to investigate some of the following career areas found in the publishing world:

- marketing
- promotion
- publicity
- corporate administration
- advertising
- production
- public relations

Earning a Living in the Book Business

The book publishing industry is definitely not a get-rich-quick place to work. Entry-level employees are not highly paid relative to their education levels. According to a 2007 survey in *Publishers Weekly*, editors with fewer than three years of experience earn an average of $30,100. Editorial personnel in the high-priced Mid-Atlantic region earn an average of $51,000. In Canada, entry-level jobs in publishing may pay as little as CAN$22,000 per year.

Furthermore, because most of the book publishing industry is centered in large metropolitan areas, your climb up the ladder will involve paying a premium price for your living quarters. Remembering that your salary should increase a little with each rung of the ladder and that you are working with books should help bookworms overcome the negatives of careers in book publishing.

....

Preparing for a Career in Book Publishing

Working in book publishing may not always be well paid, but it is an exciting field that many college graduates want to enter. There is strong competition for entry-level jobs, especially at major publishing houses. You will need a college degree. You will also need to excel in your use of the English language. A strong computer background that includes keyboarding and editing abilities is important.

Getting experience by working with books in some capacity will make you a stronger candidate for a job. Working part-time in a bookstore or library can be helpful, and finding a part-time job with a publishing house is even better because you can then show actual work experience in the industry. Working as an intern at a publishing company will also strengthen your resume. Both part-time jobs and internships can lead to job offers because they let publishing companies become acquainted with your work. You can find out what internships are available by looking at directories in libraries and online websites listing internships.

Attending book publishing courses, conferences, workshops, and seminars will increase your insight into what the industry is like. Reading *Publishers Weekly* in print or online (www .publishersweekly.com) will let you know what is happening in publishing. It is also smart to become acquainted with the *Literary Market Place* (LMP), available in most library reference sections and online (www.literarymarketplace.com). This directory lists the names, addresses, and phone numbers of book publishers in the United States and Canada. The publishers are even classified by subject matter. You will also find information about book courses, conferences, and events. There are lists of literary agents, book clubs, and foreign publishers, as well as information about acquisitions and mergers in the industry. *Writer's Market* also gives you the basic information you need to know about publishers. You can visit this website at www.writersmarket.com.

A Glimpse into the Future

The book publishing industry is likely to grow more slowly than it has in the past. Nevertheless, several types of publishing should see increased growth. The textbook segment should grow as the population of high school and college students increases as well as the need to implement new learning standards in the classroom. Plus, technical and scientific books also will be needed to relay new discoveries to the public. New opportunities for bookworms will also emerge in the area of nonprint formats for books, including e-books and audio books.

For Further Reading

Isn't it ironic that one of the best ways to prepare for a career in book publishing is by reading to learn all you can about the industry? As Lord Chesterfield once wrote, "The best companions are the best books." The following books should become your companions if you are serious about learning more about a career in book publishing.

Anderson, Jeff. *Everyday Editing: Inviting Students to Develop Skills and Craft in Writer's Workshop.* Portland, ME: Stenhouse Publishers, 2007.

Einsohn, Amy. *The Copyeditor's Handbook: A Guide for Book Publishing and Corporate Communications,* 2nd ed. Berkeley, CA: University of California Press, 2005.

Herman, Jeff. *Writer's Guide to Book Publishers, Editors, and Literary Agents 2008,* 18th ed. Stockbridge, MA: Three Dog Press, 2007.

Staff. *The Chicago Manual of Style,* 15th ed. Chicago: University of Chicago Press, 2003.

CHAPTER FOUR

Magazine and Newspaper Careers

Answering the Need for the Latest Information

Bookworms simply can't stop reading. But they definitely do not spend all their time reading books. They read magazines and newspapers, too, to find out what is happening in the world. In fact, newspapers bring such up-to-date information that many teachers call them living textbooks. This is true also for weekly newsmagazines. Both newspapers and magazines are also read for their entertainment value, from newspaper comics and humor columns to magazines devoted to the latest on what celebrities are doing. Just a few short years ago, bookworms held magazines and newspapers in their hands as they read them in such places as planes and trains, the beach, doctor's offices, and their homes. There's a new kid on the block—the online magazines and newspapers that can be read on all kinds of devices, from computers to cell phones to personal digital assistants (PDAs). Bookworms can now read magazines and newspapers just about anywhere in the world, from Tibet to Timbuktu.

People actually read newspapers before they ever started reading magazines, as magazines developed from newspapers. The original reason for having magazines was to review books, while newspapers concentrated more on news. Both early magazines and newspapers looked much the same and were held together by folds. The difference was that newspapers had numerous folds, while magazines only had one. Because magazines fell apart easily, they were soon bound.

While today some magazines and newspapers may still look the same, most magazines differ from newspapers in these obvious ways:

- higher grade of paper
- distinctive covers
- more varied typefaces
- more color illustrations
- different writing style
- more white space

Both newspapers and magazines have many jobs that require considerable reading. By finding out more about what jobs are like at each of these publications, bookworms can decide which is a better career fit for their personalities.

A Closer Look at Magazines

Publications bound in paper covers that appear regularly and contain stories, articles, and illustrations by various contributors are usually called magazines. Magazines are also called periodicals, publications, journals, reviews, newsletters, and even, occasionally, books. So, whenever you see one of these words in a want ad, you may be looking at an advertisement for a job on a magazine.

Join the staff of a magazine, and you are joining a long list of literary greats. Throughout the history of magazines, many well-known authors worked on magazine staffs, contributed articles to magazines, and even started magazines. Charles Dickens, Washington Irving, Oliver Wendell Holmes, Ralph Waldo Emerson, and Henry Adams were all involved in some way with magazines.

The Size of the Magazine Publishing Industry

There were more than fifteen thousand magazines in North America where bookworms could work in 2007. Just look at the following statistics to see where these jobs were found, according to MediaFinder.com:

U.S. magazines	13,877
Canadian magazines	1,962
U.S. online-only magazines	394
Canadian online-only magazines	43

Furthermore, each year several hundred new magazines are started. In 2007, almost four hundred new magazines were launched, according to MediaFinder.com. At the top of this list were regional magazines, followed by luxury magazines. Bookworms may find it interesting to learn that the fastest growing category of magazines is bridal magazines. Many of these are regional publications.

Unfortunately, only a handful of new magazines last, as this is a tough market to crack. Benjamin Franklin couldn't make it with his *General Magazine*, and many prominent old magazines have folded. But in spite of all the competition, some magazines, such as *People*, do succeed quite sensationally.

A Closer Look at Job Possibilities

Just walk into any drugstore, bookstore, or even the grocery store and check out the magazine racks. It won't take longer than a few minutes to discover that there are magazines on almost any subject that you can think of, from coin collecting to family health. Most of these fall into the category of consumer magazines. The other large category is business publications, which are trade, technical, and professional magazines. There are jobs for bookworms in both categories. You can work at a small magazine publisher—publishing just one magazine—or a large house that may publish as many as one hundred different magazines.

Consumer Magazines

The circulations and revenues of consumer magazines far exceed those of the greater number of trade, technical, and professional magazines. Only a small number of consumer magazines deal with general interests; most are devoted to specialized topics. Job seekers who want to work on magazines appealing to general interests usually have degrees in journalism or English. Obtaining a job on magazines with very large circulations can be quite competitive. Experience will count in getting one of these jobs.

On the other hand, if you want to work for a specialized consumer magazine, such as one dealing with computers, needlework, motorcycles, crafts, dancing, or antiques, you definitely need some knowledge or experience in that area. You are not going to get a job at a specialized computer magazine—an area with hundreds of magazines—unless you know what bytes, bits, crashing, spam, and control keys are. Nor will you be a good candidate for a job with a motorcycle magazine if you have never put on a helmet and ridden on a motorcycle.

Still, being a bookworm can help you get a job with a specialized magazine if you have done in-depth reading in the area it covers. You can find lists of all the consumer magazines that are currently being published by looking at one of the magazine directories at the end of this chapter.

Trade, Technical, and Professional Magazines

You won't usually find trade, technical, and professional magazines on magazine racks. You might find one in a doctor's, lawyer's, or accountant's office because many of these publications deal with professions. Just think of any profession; there is probably one or more magazines dealing exclusively with that field. The medical profession has an impressive list of close to one thousand magazines.

What do you think *Furniture Magazine, Automotive Magazine, Solar Today,* and *Bank News* have in common? They bring information to people who are interested in what is happening in these industries. Scarcely an industry in the United States does not have a magazine. Advertising, tobacco, welding, railroads, textiles, travel, sewage disposal, coal mining, bicycles, and luggage all have magazines, to name just a few industries.

To work on certain trade, technical, and professional magazines, you need academic training in a specific area. People working on medical magazines need to have a scientific or health care background. In other areas, it helps to be knowledgeable about a particular profession or industry; but it is not always essential. You can learn about the field through on-the-job training. Fortunately, bookworms are willing to learn through reading, too.

Editorial Jobs with Magazines

Employees on the editorial side do a lot of reading. Perhaps the better workplace for a bookworm is a consumer magazine or a magazine for a particular profession. Jobs at these magazines involve more reading because most of the material is being written by outside authors or people within a profession. This means that articles and stories will have to be considered for acquisition and copyedited—both jobs that require considerable reading. If you work for a business magazine that publishes information about an industry, it is likely that you will be doing more writing than reading because many of these magazines are written primarily in-house.

The size of the magazine determines the kind of job you are likely to have. If you work for one of the giants in the magazine industry, your job will usually be in one specific area. Work for a magazine with a staff of thirty or forty people, and your job description will be considerably broader. If you really want to be a jack-of-all-trades, get a job on a magazine that has an editorial staff of only one or two people.

The Pecking Order on a Magazine Staff

There really is not much difference between the organization charts of book publishing companies and most magazine publishers. The size of the magazine dictates how many different rungs the editorial ladder will have. What an employee does at any particular job varies from one magazine to another.

Editor in Chief or Editor. Standing on the top rung of the ladder is the editor in chief, who is responsible for the editorial content of the magazine. A person in this position must delegate many responsibilities to other members of the staff.

Managing Editor. Reporting directly to the editor in chief, a managing editor supervises daily activities at the magazine. The managing editor's job also entails supervising the staff and freelance writers, as well as writing and editing personal projects. The larger the magazine, the greater the number of assistant editors reporting to the managing editor. Most managing editors rise through the editorial ranks.

Senior, Associate, Assistant, and Specialty Editors. Depending on the size and organization of a magazine, you will find senior editors, associate editors, copyeditors, and assistant editors. Many of these editors are specialists in certain fields—such as fashion, travel, or politics—and may be called fashion editor, travel editor, political editor, and so forth. All of these editors do some reading; however, out of this group, the copyeditor is the one doing the most reading.

Editorial Assistant. Editorial assistant is an entry-level position in which you learn not only about how a magazine is put out, but also how to handle various tasks, from copyediting to acquisition.

Starting at the Bottom of the Ladder

With a recent degree in journalism in hand, Leigh Davis started her career working as an editorial assistant at the *Saturday Evening Post*. She regards this job as a wonderful beginning for an eager bookworm.

Leigh feels that it is difficult to get a job in magazine publishing and that more than a degree is needed. She has found that experience counts and thinks that her work on the college newspaper really helped her get this job. Even having worked on a high school newspaper staff would be helpful experience on a job seeker's resume.

Leigh's beginning job on the editorial side required a lot of reading. First of all, she spent a brief period of time every day reading through other general magazines to see what trends these magazines were following, especially in their travel sections.

Approximately one-third of Leigh's day was spent reading and researching as a fact-checker. For example, after checking the facts on a travel story on South Padre Island, she researched for general information on other barrier islands. Then she added some of these facts to the travel story.

Another job that took a considerable portion of Leigh's time was reading unsolicited manuscripts. A select few were forwarded to editors as possibilities for later publication.

Copyediting, however, is what took up most of Leigh's time in this job. Not only did she have to read and proofread entire articles, she even had to do quite a bit of rewriting on them. What was left of Leigh's day was spent doing clerical tasks, such as sending manuscript guidelines to freelance authors and responding to authors' questions about where their manuscripts were. Because the staff at the *Saturday Evening Post* was quite small, Leigh had the opportunity to work in several different areas, something she feels she would not have been able to do at a larger magazine.

Editor of a Parenting Publication

Twenty-five years ago, there were fewer than a handful of Parenting Publications magazines in North America. Today, there are more than two hundred. They are regional publications—usually published monthly. Their contents include articles on a variety of parenting topics, from education to health and safety to family and holiday celebrations. They typically have a calendar of events for families in the community, lots of family-centered ads, and may have book, video game, or movie reviews. These publications range in circulation from 10,000 to more than 150,000, will have from 8 to 150 pages, and are distributed free in libraries, grocery stores, drugstores, kiddie stores, public and private schools, toy stores, and wherever parents are likely to be found.

Carolyn Moore founded the third *Parents' Monthly Magazine* in the United States in Sacramento, California, in 1982. The first issue had eight pages, and she distributed the three thousand copies herself. Today, the publication can have as many as sixty-four pages, and the forty-five thousand copies are distributed in more than sixteen hundred locations throughout the metropolitan Sacramento area. With a background in typesetting and layout, Carolyn actually created every part of the first magazines, from editorial content to typesetting. With the success of the magazine as well as the advent of the computer, her job has become much easier. Today, a freelancer prepares the content for printing, and distribution and circulation are handled by her staff. Carolyn still does most of the editorial work, with the help of a freelance copyeditor.

Like all editors, Carolyn is a reader—now almost entirely on the computer. She studies the content of other parenting publications and reads all the materials that come in from freelance authors and those who have been asked to write articles before sending them on to the copyeditor. Her goal is always to make her publication a better magazine, so she is involved in every aspect of it. This includes marketing, coordinating community projects, maintaining the website, and especially planning ahead. Carolyn likes to know what articles she will be using from three to six months in the future. This involves contacting freelancers who regularly write for the magazine or who want to write for it. Being the editor of your own magazine is a challenging job; however, it is also an extremely satisfying one.

Executive Editor of a Trade Magazine

Don't just think of working for consumer magazines—there are far more trade magazines, and they may offer higher pay and greater job security. Corinna Petry is the executive editor at a conglomerate that publishes more than one hundred trade magazines. She is in charge of a magazine, website, and electronic newsletter for one trade brand. She spends most of her day in front of a computer—editing, writing, and reporting on events in the financial services industry. Corinna especially enjoys her job because she likes to crunch numbers and has the opportunity to do a lot of financial analysis. An associate editor and an art director help her produce these publications.

Starting Out as a Reporter. With a degree in journalism and an internship at a medium-size newspaper, Corinna was well-prepared to secure a job after graduating from college. She answered an ad and found her first job at a pro-union labor newspaper with only two employees and the owner. Corinna gained valuable experience here as she wrote copy, typeset, and even sold ads.

Moving from Newspapers to Trade Magazines. Corinna's next two jobs were at community newspapers, where she worked as a reporter and copyeditor. Then she began to get experience in business trade journalism by becoming a reporter on a daily (five times a week) newspaper covering the metals industry. Her first magazine job was as the managing editor of a metals trade magazine, where her editorial responsibilities included managing the production flow of the magazine plus writing and editing news and features. All of her experience in business reporting and magazines helped Corinna secure her current job. She found it online and also knew someone who worked at the company.

Letters Department Manager

Other jobs on magazine staffs require considerable reading. Ken Porter, manager of the letters department at a national newsmagazine, has one of those jobs. Roughly a thousand letters arrive by e-mail or fax at this very popular publication each week. Ken and his staff—many with master's degrees in journalism—have the responsibility of handling these letters. The letters first go to a clerk, who determines where they will be routed. Some are forwarded to other departments. The remaining letters are distributed to the staff of the letters department for reply.

A great number of the letters are routine and can be answered by form letters or slightly adapted form letters. Others require original replies, often necessitating some research. These letters must be accurate because they reflect the views of the editors of the newsmagazine. The letters correspondents often need to consult with the author of an article for help in drafting a reply.

Each week, one of the staff members sorts through all the letters and divides them into groups that reflect the stories they are commenting on and the viewpoints of the letter writers. Then Ken and some of his staff select the letters to be used in the letters column. Many letters must be edited for reasons of clarity and space. Ken also adds editor's comments when necessary.

Ken believes that reading letters is an excellent way to start at this newsmagazine. Not only does this job have the fringe benefit that you might be noticed, it also provides valuable experience in editing, researching, and writing—skills essential to journalism. Ken started in the entry-level position of letter correspondent and is now the manager of the letters department. Before getting his first job in this department, it was necessary for Ken to pass a test demonstrating his ability to write clear, conversational prose.

Getting Your Foot in the Door

No one, perfect route guarantees a job with a magazine. Certainly, a liberal arts degree seems to be a starting point for most people working on the editorial side of magazine publishing. Experience with a publication—from high school newspaper to college literary magazine—is also helpful. Even a little experience lets a prospective magazine employee write down something in the spaces asking for experience on application forms.

Having an internship on a magazine is another excellent way to get the experience job hunters need. Some internships are part-time jobs during the school year in which students receive academic credit and no money. There are also summer programs that offer some pay. You will find that most publishers have intern programs for undergraduates and recent graduates.

The reference section of the library has many directories listing internships. Before you sign up for an internship program, make sure that it is project oriented and that you know exactly what you will be doing. Twelve weeks of meaningless clerical work could seem like an eternity. It can also be helpful to select an internship at a firm where you would later like to work. Another avenue in preparing for a job in magazine publishing is attending a writing course during the summer.

The First Steps as an Intern

Jennie Duffy, a recent college graduate in communications, wants to find a job on a weekly lifestyle magazine. She needs solid recommendations from an employer in this area, experience in working on a magazine, and samples of her work to show prospective employers. Jennie hopes to fill these needs through a three-month internship with Diablo Publications, working on the firm's *Diablo* magazine, a lifestyle magazine in Northern California. As an intern, she has been able to do some writing and is spending time researching and fact-checking. Because the internship only pays a modest stipend, Jennie has two other jobs in order to support herself. Nevertheless, Jennie is optimistic that she is on the way to a career with a magazine.

The Magazine Pay Scale

Starting out on the editorial side of the magazine industry will give you much the same income as starting in the book publishing industry. Most entry-level positions average slightly more than $30,000 a year in the United States. How much editors make depends greatly on their years of experience. Salaries range from $39,000 to more than $70,000. In Canada, the average salary for editors is slightly more than CAN$44,000. At all levels, you will make more working for trade, technical, and professional magazines than at consumer magazines. You will also make more money at magazines with larger circulations. If you are working on a magazine in the Northeast United States or a large city in Canada, you will earn more than if you work in other areas. Unfortunately, it also costs more to live in these places.

Your Future in the Magazine Industry

Overall, the number of print magazines is expected to continue growing, especially regional and narrow niche magazines, increasing job opportunities for bookworms. Another bright spot for job seekers is that the number of Web-based magazines is also increasing. Plus, larger print magazines need additional staff for their online editions. While some pessimists believe the number of magazines will decline in the near future, most members of the industry see it as one that will continue to grow.

A Look at the Newspaper Industry

The first printed newspaper was distributed during the eighth century in China. Even earlier, newspapers were handwritten and posted in public places. One of these was the *Acta Diurna*, meaning "daily events," which actually started in Rome in 59 B.C.

Benjamin Harris of Boston founded the first newspaper in the United States in 1690. It was called the *Publick Occurrences Both Forreign and Domestick* and had an extraordinarily brief history because the government stopped it after the first issue. The 1800s were the heyday for the development of newspapers. The largest number of newspapers ever in the United States was about twenty-six hundred dailies in 1909. Today, the number of daily newspapers is less than fifteen hundred.

The first newspaper in Canada, the *Halifax Gazette*, was published in 1752 by John Bushell, a printer from Boston. As more and more settlers arrived after 1800, the number of newspapers grew. Today, there are slightly more than one hundred daily newspapers in Canada.

The Newspaper Circulation Story

In North America, newspaper circulation is currently falling. The greatest declines have occurred in large metro newspapers. Much of this has been attributed to the defection of readers to the Internet and other media. See if you can identify the three newspapers with the largest circulations in the United States today from the following list:

- *Wall Street Journal*
- *New York Times*
- *Chicago Tribune*

- *Washington Post*
- *Los Angeles Times*
- *Miami Herald*
- *USA Today*
- *Denver Post/Rocky Mountain News*

Your first choice should have been *USA Today*, followed by the *Wall Street Journal* and the *New York Times*. The largest newspaper in Canada is the *Toronto Star*.

The *USA Today* Story

USA Today was founded in 1982. It is now the second largest newspaper in the world. The only larger paper is the *Times of India*. The goal behind launching *USA Today* was to give the United States a national newspaper. It features easy-to-read stories and an atypical layout. All of the front page stories are complete on that page, except for the cover story, and a state-by-state roundup of headlines is featured in each edition. It was one of the first newspapers in the country to send satellite transmissions to locations across the country for printing and distribution.

Lifestyle Editor at a Daily Newspaper

Adrienne Mauk, the lifestyle and special sections editor for the *Lima News* in Lima, Ohio, has always been a bookworm. She started reading before kindergarten and devoured all the Nancy Drew books one after another as fast as she could in elementary school. Reading has always been in her brain, as she puts it, as well as writing. Because she is a planner, she began to think as a teenager of how she could have a word-oriented career, quickly deciding that working on a newspaper or magazine could be the right choice for her.

Career Preparation. Adrienne began her formal study of journalism in junior high school, at the school's TV news program, and then enrolled in a college that had a strong journalism program. She focused on newspapers, which offer everyday practice in becoming a better writer, and worked as an intern at a small newspaper during college for three summers. While she didn't earn a lot of money, she gained invaluable experience filling in for vacationing staff members. As an intern, Adrienne did a lot of writing, designing, typing, and interviewing for articles. She considered this experience a valuable addition to what she had learned in her journalism classes at college. Later, she interned at an arts magazine near her college and worked part-time there during school. She wrote a few stories there but mainly worked on proofreading and fact-checking—other valuable skills to have. After graduation, she had a summer internship at a major Ohio newspaper, where she wrote stories and learned how a large newspaper works.

Finding a Job. Ten years ago, the Internet was not the important job search tool that it is today. So, after graduating from college, Adrienne phoned just about every medium to large paper in her home state asking if they had any jobs. Fortunately, several were hiring. After interviewing, she decided to take a position as a features writer at the *Lima News* and is still there today. It is important to note what a strong background Adrienne had for getting this position because of her experience on her internships and her degree in journalism.

Moving up the Career Ladder. Once you have a job, Adrienne points out, you have the opportunity to show your bosses that you want to learn. This will make them excited about you, and soon you will be moving up the career ladder at a rapid rate. And this is exactly what Adrienne did. After spending several years writing for entertainment and then health departments, Adrienne applied for the position of lifestyle editor when there was a vacancy and got the job.

An Editor's Job. While all days are different for Adrienne as a lifestyle editor, there is one constant—she reads all the time, mostly in front of a computer. She reads stories by local reporters, wire stories, news releases, other papers, and loads of e-mail. Because she has to do so much reading as part of planning what will be in the lifestyle section, it is very helpful that she is a fast reader. Adrienne, like most editors, does not have a nine-to-five job. Instead, she comes into the newspaper at about ten and stays until six or seven on Monday through Thursday—sometimes later, depending on the task at hand. Then on Friday, she works on the city desk—editing hard news—from three in the afternoon until midnight. She also has the responsibility of being the special sections editor and puts out a section almost every week on such topics as weddings, education, and special events. There is certainly no opportunity to get bored! These responsibilities, beyond being the lifestyle editor, are typical for editors at smaller papers. Hers has a circulation of forty thousand readers.

Career Advice. Adrienne believes that it is very important to begin looking at career options as a teen. Then she advises you to go after what you want to do because a good job doesn't just happen to you. And, she adds, "Don't let rejection letters bother you because everyone has a collection of them."

A Varied Career as a Newspaper Editor

The climb to the top in the newspaper publishing industry is very similar to that in the book and magazine industries. Dennis Hetzel is a bookworm who has gone from writing for a local paper while still in high school to being the general manager of the *Kentucky Enquirer* in Fort Mitchell, Kentucky, with a wide range of editorial jobs in between. Dennis has received many personal honors for his work in the newspaper industry. He believes that it is essential to read in order to succeed in this industry.

Starting Out in Newspaper Publishing. Dennis began his newspaper career in high school. Not being able to excel in sports, Dennis coupled his love of sports with his writing ability and freelanced as a sports reporter for the local weekly. He majored in political science and minored in journalism in college and had plans to become a high school teacher—he even did his student teaching. However, an opportunity to become the sports editor for two weekly papers changed his career path. He believes that his high school sports writing experience got him this job. Working in sports, according to Dennis, requires a tremendous amount of reading each day just to keep track of what is happening.

After a year, Dennis went to another paper in Galesburg, Illinois, as a reporter. On this paper, one of his beats was the courts, which required the ability to read fast and to read for understanding. Dennis had to review lengthy, complicated documents and determine the important points.

Climbing the Editorial Ladder. After taking a job as a reporter with another paper in Racine, Wisconsin, Dennis became special projects editor within a few years. He did a lot of research on this job; he read and edited others' work and researched special projects. Continuing his upward climb, Dennis became an associate editor. This job required him to supervise the copy desk and prepare the front page. He had to read stories coming in from outside news services and pick out the ones to use in the paper. Several hundred stories might be available, while there was room for only a few dozen.

Advancing to Managing Editor. In 1986, Dennis became managing editor of the *Capital Times* in Madison, Wisconsin. Half or more of his time was spent on managerial tasks. He read and wrote many memos, but he also read newspapers and articles in trade magazines such as *Editor & Publisher*. Besides reading his own newspaper, he read two or three other newspapers every morning, plus an afternoon newspaper.

Becoming Editor and Publisher. In 1990, Dennis took the job as editor and publisher of the *York Daily Record*. As publisher, he was the chief operating officer and played more of a role in community affairs. As editor, he was responsible for setting the overall policy and direction of the newspaper. Dennis continued to read several newspapers a day; however, he soon found that he was reading more online and seeing a migration away from print.

Serving as General Manager of a Local Newspaper. In 2004, Dennis was named manager of the *Kentucky Enquirer*. His goal was to build the paper into an even better local morning paper while making its online presence stronger. His online responsibility shows how the newspaper world is changing from a print-only format.

A Copyeditor's Job

Copyediting requires on-the-job reading—not for just part of the day, but all day, every workday. Copyediting is the process of reviewing and editing the work of reporters so it is ready for layout. It involves correcting spelling, grammar, and punctuation errors. Copyediting on a magazine or a book may involve fact-checking, but copy is generally considered correct by the time it gets to the copyeditor. There just isn't time on a newspaper for a copyeditor to check facts beyond looking for obvious errors or inconsistencies.

Jim Lindgren is features copy desk chief in charge of eleven copyeditors at a major newspaper in the Midwest. At the start of the day, thirty or forty stories may be stored in the newspaper's computer system waiting to be edited. Reporters have written the stories and given them to their editors, who may have made some changes. Then the page designers place instructions on the stories detailing what kind of headlines are to be used and what the size of the story should be (column length). These stories are then assigned to rim editors by the slot editor, who parcels out assignments and makes sure that the copyeditors are working on what is needed. At most newspapers, all this is done by computer.

Jim pulls a story up on his computer monitor, and the copyediting process begins. According to journalism textbooks, stories should be read through completely before doing any editing. With the time restraints of newspaper deadlines, however, this doesn't happen all the time. As Jim reads through the copy, he edits. For an experienced copyeditor like Jim, the errors usually jump out. He knows what words are often misspelled and even what mistakes individual reporters make.

At times, Jim must do considerable rewriting to meet space specifications, which are sometimes so tight that he might substitute the word *try* for *attempt*. At the press of a button on his computer, Jim can tell whether the story is the correct length. When a story is the correct size, he writes a headline that tells the story and meets the space allotted for it. The story is then sent to the slot editor, who reads through it and approves the editing and headline.

Once all the stories on a page are completed, a proof is made, and it is read to check for mistakes. When any mistakes have been corrected, the page is ready to appear in the paper.

When the first copies of the paper come out, Jim and the other copyeditors read through it and note any needed corrections on the paper. New stories in subsequent editions are also checked for errors.

Personal Qualifications of Copyeditors. You must have a love affair with words. You should enjoy playing with words. Most copyeditors are confirmed punsters. They also work crosswords, as Jim does, to learn smaller words for larger words. Above all, you need to be a bookworm who enjoys reading a wide variety of material both on and off the job. Jim met this qualification as a child—he always had his nose in adventure books.

Copyeditors typically have bachelor's degrees in English or journalism. Jim's is in journalism. In college, he worked on the student newspaper, which gave him experience in reporting, editing, and design and helped him discover that he enjoyed editing most of all. He advises future copyeditors to get a foot in the door by being willing to take any job that allows them to work for a paper. He began his career as editor of a small-town weekly paper and then began copyediting at a small daily paper before moving to his present newspaper to begin the climb up the copyediting ladder.

Bookworms must realize that copyeditors do not sit in soft easy chairs leisurely editing. At most newspapers, they sit in front of computers staring at stories on monitors for hours. The pace is quite fast, as they hurry to get copy ready to be printed. Perhaps one of the best ways to determine if copyediting is for you is to read the requirements for a copyediting job on a large metropolitan newspaper with a circulation of several hundred thousand.

The Newspaper Pay Scale

No matter where your first job is in publishing, you will not be earning a high starting salary. The average salary for all newspaper editors in the United States is slightly more than $44,000 and more than CAN$48,000 in Canada. In both countries, salaries are considerably higher on larger newspapers.

Getting a Foot in the Door

You are most likely to get your first job in the newspaper industry because a reporter or copyeditor has left the industry, been promoted, or moved to a larger newspaper. Competition for jobs on major newspapers is fierce. Small-town and suburban papers offer better opportunities for finding that all-important first job. No matter where you get your first job, you are likely to be working for a newspaper chain because chains own the majority of newspapers in both the United States and Canada.

To get just about any entry-level job on a newspaper, you must have excellent word-processing skills. Computer graphics and desktop publishing skills may also be useful. Most employers will expect you to have a bachelor's degree in journalism, but some hire graduates with other majors. Experience is very important in getting a job. It is just about essential to be able to list an internship, part-time job, or summer job in the industry to secure your first newspaper job. It even helps to have worked on your high school or college newspaper.

Your Future in the Newspaper Industry

The employment picture in the newspaper industry is bleak right now, especially for paper editions. Circulation is falling, and advertisers are leaving daily papers to run ads online on a wide variety of websites. This is a serious problem as it's advertisements that produce profits for newspapers. To increase profits, newspapers, especially those that are part of large chains, are cutting staff in order to raise profit margins. Some pessimists actually see the demise of newspapers within the next fifty years—expecting people to rely almost entirely on the Internet and television for all of their information needs.

A more realistic view is the transformation of the newspaper as we now know it. Just as we have e-books, there is now talk of e-newspapers. In the future, some see people getting the latest-breaking news online from newspaper websites and traditional papers evolving more into newsmagazines. The key to the continued success of newspapers lies in their recapturing a large share of the online advertising market, launching niche publications, and reaching out to new audiences. All of the bloggers in the world will never produce the reliable information, especially news, that newspapers provide. Online editions of papers are likely to grow and become the daily newspaper, especially for the younger segment of the population. Fortunately, they will still need staff to write and edit them.

One bright spot at the present time is the community newspaper. The circulation of many of these papers is growing. This is because people want to know what is going on where they live, from local concerns to social events to school news to nearby store advertisements.

For bookworms, newspapers are an appealing career choice even if the traditional newspapers are changing. Of course, not every employee reads for eight hours a day, but most do some reading. Furthermore, positions like copyeditor and wire editor offer almost eight hours a day of reading.

Two Satisfying Careers for Bookworms

What do people working on magazines and newspapers have in common? They usually love the work they do. They thrive on the excitement of deadlines, whether they are the deadlines for different editions of a newspaper or the weekly, monthly, or quarterly deadlines of magazines. While they garner satisfaction from providing information so that people can know what is going on around them, they universally complain about low pay. Most of all, they savor working with words in some way.

For Further Reading

If you are seeking employment with a magazine or newspaper, it is a good idea to look at directories that list the large number of companies in this field. All kinds of interesting job possibilities exist. You might find it possible to combine your interest in birds or clothing with working on a consumer specialty magazine. Perhaps your addiction to reading about current events would be satisfied through working on an online newspaper. Information in the following books should be helpful:

Directories

Bacon's Magazine Directory. Chicago: Cision, annual.

Bacon's Newspaper Directory. Chicago: Cision, annual.

The Directory of Small Press & Magazine Editors & Publishers. Paradise, CA: Dustbooks, biannual.

Editor & Publisher International Year Book. New York: Editor & Publisher, annual.

National Directory of Magazines: Comprehensive Presentation of U.S. and Canadian Magazines. New York: Oxbridge Communications, annual.

Writer's Market. Cincinnati, OH: F+W Publications, annual.

Books

Careers in Focus: Newspapers. New York: Ferguson Publishing, 2007.

Careers in Focus: Publishing, 3rd ed. New York: Ferguson Publishing, 2007.

Johnson, Sammye, and Patricia Prijatel. *The Magazine from Cover to Cover: Inside a Dynamic Industry.* New York: McGraw-Hill, 2006.

Yager, Fred, and Jan Yager. *Career Opportunities in the Publishing Industry.* New York: Facts on File, 2005.

CHAPTER FIVE

Internet Career Opportunities

Working Online with Bookworms

t's a Web world now. Just a few years ago, computers were only for work. Now people spend hours in front of them having fun, from playing games to chatting with family and friends. The Internet has brought other changes, too. If you're under fifty, it's quite likely that you are now getting your news online instead of from paper publications. And if you are a student researching a term paper, you are more likely to go online than to the library. The Internet is rapidly opening an abundance of new careers for bookworms—some that could not have been imagined just a few years ago. So when you think of an online career that would involve a lot of reading, you need to realize that there are far more options than working on the website of a magazine or newspaper.

Jobs in Information Services

Among the fastest-growing businesses in the economy are the information services companies that generate, process, and distribute data. With the world just about drowning in information, businesses, schools, professional people, the government, and even students researching papers need help to find information quickly. And this demand for information continues to accelerate each year, especially as more and more information is placed on the Internet.

Information services professionals get paid to read about the arts, environment, photography, and many other topics. Many work as indexers and abstractors for information services companies, where they read journals, magazines, and newspapers; organize bibliographic information; and write abstracts for articles. Writing an abstract involves reflecting the author's opinion. Many companies have a training period for this job during which employees learn editorial policy, what goes into abstracts, how to organize and select material, and how to avoid plagiarism. Of course, you have to love to read to enjoy this job. Other job requirements include a college degree, expertise in grammar, computer literacy, and an ability to record information accurately.

At some information services companies, you must work on-site. Others let you work at home and send your work in electronically. Although there are deadlines, you are often free to structure the hours you work. This flexibility makes the job appealing to many people, and the nature of the work itself is perfectly suited to bookworms.

Working as an Abstractor and Indexer

Callie Johnson loves her job because this bookworm gets paid to read for an information services company. And she gets to read a lot of things that she enjoys. Plus, she doesn't even have to work in an office because this freelancer is able to work from her home in the foothills of California. Newspapers, journals, and newsletters are sent to her so she can organize abstracts and bibliographic information about them for an academic database. To get this job, she had to take a test to demonstrate how well she could write. Callie can work whenever she wants; however, she does have to meet deadlines.

As an abstractor, it is Callie's job to represent what an author says in a very abbreviated form. She must do this well so customers of the company will know whether or not they want to read an article. To be successful in this area, you must be able to work fast. She can do two to four whole magazines in a day or an entire paper following the selection guidelines of her employer. Not every article in a publication will require abstracts. For some, she only writes the bibliographic and key subject terms.

Bookworms as Internet Entrepreneurs

Here are three stories of how book lovers have created careers by bringing their unique ideas to the world via the Internet.

A Website for Bookworms

Once upon a time, bookworms simply displayed their hundreds or even thousands of books in shelves in their homes for fellow book lovers to explore at their leisure. Thanks to LibraryThing (www.librarything.com), created by Tim Spalding, it's now possible to display your collection online for anyone in the world to see. LibraryThing provides you with a way to catalog your personal library. It lets you use the Dewey Decimal or Library of Congress systems or tag your books with your own subjects to organize your collection. Members of this website enter the ISBN number, author, or title of a book. Then LibraryThing searches the Library of Congress, Amazon.com sites, and more than two hundred world libraries and returns with precise data about the book. You can then add the information to your own personal online catalog of books.

LibraryThing not only offers a way to display your book collection to others, it also gives you the opportunity to connect with people who have similar libraries. It also makes book recommendations based on the collective intelligence of the other libraries. Plus, you can connect with like-minded readers in a sort of MySpace for bookworms to chat about books.

Since its founding in 2005, more than twenty-two million books have been cataloged on the LibraryThing website. It is very popular with bookworms as more than 340,000 users have signed up. Of this number, from 50,000 to 60,000 are regular users. The success of LibraryThing has led to other sites that imitate it. You will not find a lot of employees at this website company, however. At present, there are only the developer and founder and seven employees. All are definitely bookworms, and most were users of the site before they became employees.

Bookworms can find interesting jobs on the websites where other bookworms visit frequently. Plus, there's also always the possibility of creating your own website company that will let you work with books in some capacity every day on the job.

Tim Spalding's Career Path. Tim Spalding grew up in a house that was stuffed with books. Today, he has a library of about three thousand books, and his brother has a library twice that size. You can understand why Tim was always interested, even as a child, in organizing his books. While he was studying for his master's in Latin and Greek and working at a major book publisher, he started a project to catalog his own library and those belonging to academic and bookworm friends. Part of the reason that he became interested in cataloging online was that he found that he was buying new books that were already in his library and wanted a way to rapidly access what books he owned before making a purchase. Tim had the right background for starting an online company as he was a freelance Web developer and Web publisher. His previous projects included www.isidore-of-seville.com and www.ancientlibrary.com. However, he never imagined that LibraryThing would become more than a hobby and such a successful Web venture. He thought that the site would probably only grow to a few hundred members. Since 2006, he has partnered with Abebooks.com, an online service that connects independent booksellers to customers, and LibraryThing is continuing to grow.

Career Advice. Tim understands that fellow bookworms would want to find a career that lets them work in some way with books.

For those wanting to have a Web career, he suggests that you look for some little things that use the Web to add value to the experiences of reading, writing, publishing, and bookselling.

Internet Consultant

Margaret Dikel has a terrific job for a bookworm as much of her day involves reading. She is a private consultant working with companies, organizations, and agencies to develop their use of the Internet for career transition and job search. She is also the creator of the Riley Guide, a directory of employment and career information sources and services on the Internet. Her reading begins with the morning newspaper, where she looks for information that might be helpful to her clients or visitors to her website, www.rileyguide.com. Throughout the day, she reads library and trade journals and electronic newsletters and visit websites for news and information when she is not working with clients or updating her website.

This bookworm has indeed carved out a career combining the fascination of the online world with a lot of reading. It is an excellent choice for Margaret, whose fascination with books led her to become a library aide in elementary school, high school, and college. After earning a master's degree in library and information sciences, she worked for thirteen years in academic libraries before striking out on her own more than ten years ago.

Career Advice. Margaret points out that job seekers need to know that the Internet doesn't answer all of your job needs. It is a great place for finding out what jobs are out there and offers a quick way to apply for jobs, but not necessarily the best way. It is also an excellent way to find out a lot about companies and different regions of the country where you might wish to work. Margaret stresses, however, that the Net cannot take the place of meeting with people. You need to network with people—even if it is only being proactive in an Internet chat room. The downsides of limiting one's search to the Net are that too many resumes just end up in databases and that too often there is a lack of response to online job applications.

Project Gutenberg: e-Texts for Everyone

In about 1450, Johannes Gutenberg invented the printing press and changed the world. Books that once cost the equivalent of a family farm became available at a price the masses could afford. In a similar way, Michael Hart, as founder of Project Gutenberg, has changed the world by making more than one hundred thousand books available for free on the Internet at www.gutenberg.org, www.gutenberg.cc, www.gutenberg.ca, and many other international websites. It is his dream to make all literature universally available online. Between 1971 and 1993, Michael produced one hundred e-texts with the help of many who did not believe that the project would ever take off. Now, with the help of an army of close to one hundred thousand volunteers, about four hundred e-texts are being added each month. Most are scanned and then carefully proofread by volunteers. This is one volunteer job that guarantees that you will do nothing but read—an excellent choice for a bookworm.

How the Project Started. Back in 1971, Michael, then a college student, discovered that the computer facility at the University of Illinois was a great place to study because it was air-conditioned. He figured out how to run the mainframe (Xerox Sigma V) and knew it was connected to a network—part of which would become the Internet. The mainframe operator, a friend of his brother's, gave him an operator's account—$100 million worth of computer time. Michael puzzled over what to do with this bonanza and decided that he wanted to send something significant to all the people who were connected to the Net at that time—"all one hundred of them." It was July 4, 1971, and he had been given a copy of the Declaration of Independence at the grocery store. He typed in the text of the Declaration, and eventually six of the approximately hundred Net users actually downloaded it. Michael knew then that e-texts were a definite possibility. It would be seventeen years before any others agreed with him. The popularity of e-texts is now growing rapidly— fueled by the development of so many devices that let you read these books no matter where you are. Today, one of the mirror sites that Project Gutenberg set up actually gives away thirty-five million books a year—more than a book a second. The one fly in the ointment to getting more and more new books online is copyright law, which now extends the exclusive rights of authors and their families to ninety-five years, keeping millions of books out of the public domain.

The Future of the Gutenberg Project. Technology is fueling what can be done with e-texts. Michael sees the personal computer becoming your personal library. In fact, a single chip can now hold more books than the average U.S. or Canadian public library has. As executive director of Project Gutenberg, his target is "A million books to a billion people in all corners of the globe." And then his next big project is to translate ten million books into a hundred different languages for a library of a billion Project Gutenberg books.

Qualifications for Internet Jobs

Several of the careers described in this chapter resulted from individuals seeing a special need for something to be done on the Net. Tim Spalding wanted an easy way to check on the books that he owned. Margaret Dikel was the first to write a guide to using the Internet to aid in searching for a job, and Michael Hart wanted to put books online for people to read. Perhaps you will be the one to create something new that bookworms like you would like to see online.

In searching for an Internet career that will let you read a lot on the job, remember that businesses on the Net respect college degrees. A technical major is not necessary. And, of course, you can read while searching for a job online.

For Further Reading

While you can definitely find all types of information online about careers associated with the Internet, there are also many books that give a good perspective on these careers. Here are some that you may wish to read.

Bolles, Mark Emery, and Richard Nelson Bolles. *Job Hunting Online: A Guide to Using Job Listings, Message Boards, Research Sites, the Underweb*, 5th ed. Berkeley, CA: Ten Speed Press, 2008.

O'Bryan, Pat. *The Absolute Beginner's Guide to Internet Wealth.* Garden City, NY: Morgan James Publishing, 2007.

Silver, Yanik. *Moonlighting on the Internet.* Madison, WI: Entrepreneur Media, Inc., 2007.

Taylor, Allan, James Robert Parish, and Dan Fiden. *Career Opportunities in the Internet, Video Games, and Multimedia.* New York: Checkmark Books, 2007.

CHAPTER SIX

Glamorous Reading Careers

Enjoying the Public Spotlight

M any bookworms savor being in the public spotlight. You see them every day on TV and listen to them on the radio. Reading to keep current with what is going on in the world is a major part of their job, especially for news reporters and talk-show hosts. And behind them are staffs reading to provide them with additional information. There are even more behind-the-scenes jobs that involve working closely with radio, television, or movie personalities. Someone has to type, read, and analyze all the scripts submitted to television and movie companies and major stars. Public relations firms need readers to find out what others are saying about their clients in newspapers and magazines. Throughout all of these glamour industries, there are many jobs at all levels that are perfect for bookworms.

The lure of working in some way in movies, television, radio, or public relations is so great that college graduates are fiercely competing for entry-level positions. Unfortunately, first jobs in these industries generally require long and hard hours and offer low pay. Preparation for one of these jobs is, however, up a bookworm's alley: you have to read as much as you can to get an idea of the basics of how radio and television shows are produced, movies are made, and public relations campaigns are handled.

Radio—the Vocal Medium

Many people don't realize that before television became so popular, families sat around their radios every evening. They listened to "The Great Gildersleeve," "The Jack Benny Program," and "Inner Sanctum Mysteries" for entertainment. They found out about what was happening in the world by listening to Lowell Thomas, Edward R. Murrow, and other famous news commentators. Some danced to the music of the big bands or Top 40 tunes. But this golden age of radio ended when television took over.

Radio did not roll over and play dead. Instead, radio changed its format. All-talk, all-news, and all-music stations emerged, as well as stations with formats designed to attract particular audiences. Soon radio had captured more listeners than ever before. In fact, homes today have a far greater number of radios than television sets. Perhaps part of this can be traced to the convenience of radio. You can drive a car and listen to the radio. You can jog down the street listening to a radio. You can listen to radios on buses, trains, and Ferris wheels. The current popularity of radio means more jobs for people wanting to work in this medium. Many of these jobs are designed for people who love to talk and read.

"Bookworm"—a Radio Show for Book Lovers

Few careers for bookworms can be as perfect as the one Michael Silverblatt has as host of "Bookworm," a weekly public radio series heard across the United States. Unfortunately, there aren't many opportunities to have a radio talk show like his that lets you sit down and talk to an author face-to-face for thirty minutes, especially when they are well-known writers of literary fiction and poetry, such as Salman Rushdie, Amy Tan, and John Irving. The late Norman Mailer characterized Michael as "the best reader in America." And reader he definitely is—devoting at least six hours a day to reading. He's able to devote so much time as he does not have a driver's license and reads on the bus or in the backseats of friends' cars. He also wakes up in the middle of the night to read for several hours. Reading is definitely Michael's passion and has been so ever since fourth grade. And this pastime was greatly nourished while he was a student at the University of Buffalo by the extraordinary English department and its constant stream of literary greats.

Michael believes that one of the reasons you go to college is to find out what you're not good at. He discovered that he was not good at novel writing, which had been his career goal. What he was good at was reading and talking about books. By chance, he fell into a career that let him do both after working in the publishing world, in bookstores, and as a freelance writer and film publicist. The start of his career can be traced to what happened at a dinner with one of his publicist clients. Michael became very engaged in a conversation about Russian literature with a dinner companion who happened to be the general manager of KCRW-FM. The result was an offer at the end of the dinner for his own show. For the first five and a half years, it was a labor of love subsidized totally by Michael. Today, the show—now in its twentieth year—is supported by a foundation grant and has a staff of two employees.

A lot of preparation goes into making each show. The associate producer goes to the tapings with Michael and works with him on producing the show as well as with the stations carrying the show. The editor, who keeps the office running, goes through forty to eighty books a week to select possible books for Michael to use on the show. (He receives many books because of the popularity of the show.) Michael always makes the final selections—choosing books in which he finds something to admire. Then he sits down with the author for the interview and talks not just about the book, but also about such things as the author's debt to other writers or the proper use of irony in romantic and passionate passages. These unscripted conversations may last far longer than the twenty-eight minutes allowed for the show. The editor does the initial editing, and then he and Michael complete the process together. You can listen to this radio host's interviews online at www.kcrw.com.

Career Advice. Michael advises fellow bookworms not to compromise their dream of a career that involves books. He says that you must not take another job just because it is there. Great job possibilities, according to Michael, will emerge if you keep looking for them. They may even happen by accident. He found his dream job from a conversation at a dinner in Hollywood.

A Radio Talk-Show Host

You have probably listened to talk shows and may even have called in to offer your opinion on some topic. Many radio stations have an all-talk format, with hosting jobs that are perfect for bookworms. In order to host a talk show, it is absolutely essential to keep up-to-date with what is happening in the world. Barbara Simpson, the host of her own talk program on KSFO in San Francisco, loves this aspect of her job and believes it is why she can talk about anything and ad-lib with ease.

Once the calls start coming, Barbara never knows what her audience will talk about. It could be one of the topics from her opening chat or a casual remark from a listener that captures everyone's interest. Barbara spends at least thirty hours a week reading in preparation for her program.

Each month Barbara reads more than fifty-five publications, from *People* to *National Review* to the CDC's *Morbidity and Mortality Weekly Report*. Besides perusing local, regional, national, and international newspapers daily, she reads varied newswire and Internet resources. Barbara gets ideas for her program everywhere. A book review on espionage or a newspaper article on prenatal surgery may lead her to guests and show topics.

Barbara's career extends beyond the boundaries of being a talk-show host. She writes a column for WorldNetDaily.com and does media and political consulting through her company, Blue Shadow Productions.

Career Advice. If you are drawn to a career in radio, Barbara advises finding an internship so you can evaluate whether this choice is really right for you. She also recommends getting a degree in liberal arts with an academic emphasis because it gives you the broad knowledge needed to measure today's events in light of history. You also need to love to talk.

A Radio Deejay

Jeff Pigeon worked for twenty years as a radio deejay on an adult contemporary program. He was an early-morning bookworm— not a twenty-four-hour-a-day bookworm. Arriving at the station each morning at 4:15 for his 5 A.M. show, he began reading immediately. He read the local morning paper plus two other newspapers so he would know what had been happening locally and around the world when he went on the air. His producer was also busy reading, giving Jeff highlighted articles to take to the studio.

While Jeff enjoys reading, he is definitely not a speed reader. Because he likes to take his time with the printed word and slowly absorb what he is reading, he did a lot of his job-related reading at home. He always read the evening paper along with a whole list of popular magazines and even the tabloids. Jeff was also kept busy trying to keep up with all the new books that publishers sent to him. He had to resort to skimming many of these books.

Jeff was constantly preparing for his show. Everything that happened to him during the day as well as anything he read could be a good topic of conversation on one of his shows. He feels that those who want to succeed in the radio industry will read as much material as they can get their hands on.

A Radio-Show Producer

Mark Silverman is producer of the "Ronn Owens Program," which airs five mornings a week on KGO in San Francisco. This is a very popular news talk show that has people call in. Ronn, the host, interacts with the callers and also interviews guests. He is an avid reader, and so is Mark, who, as a child, actually read with a flashlight while walking his dog at night. Today, this bookworm even reads the newspaper while taking a shower.

Because Ronn's show airs in the morning, Mark regularly gets up between 5:30 and 6 A.M. so he can go through two local and two national newspapers and look at a variety of Web news sources. Then he continues reading while riding on the train to work. Mark is looking for interesting stories to complement the big-picture stories that Ronn has studied. For example, once he found a story about a grocery store clerk who apprehended a shoplifter and was subsequently fired for the way he handled a customer. When Mark arrives at the office, he reads more and gives the host his input on the list of topics for the day's show. He primarily consults with Ronn both before and during the program by computer. During the show, he screens calls, looking for people with passion and divergent views to bring balance to the show. After the show, he discusses the next day's program with Ronn.

Part of Mark's job involves reading newspapers, news and pop-culture magazines, and websites to look for good guests, as well as moral issues for Ronn's personal opinion segment at the start of the show. An added dividend to this job beside all the reading required is meeting and talking to well-known public figures who have appeared as guests. He has met Supreme Court Justice Stephen Breyer and was the producer when shock jock Howard Stern called the program to confront studio guest FCC Chairman Michael Powell.

Movies—a Glamorous Environment for Readers

The movie industry is a rather small one, with fewer than a quarter-million people working in it. If your dream is to work in this industry, you should pack your bags and head for Southern California because it's still the center of moviemaking in North America. New York is second on the list of places to work, followed by Vancouver, British Columbia. Most of the movie jobs that are ideal for bookworms center on handling scripts. Some jobs put you in touch with the stars—from handling their fan mail to reading scripts for them. Some jobs also exist in doing research to determine that everything shown in a film is as authentic as possible. Whatever your job in this industry, the possibility of meeting famous stars and directors is always there.

The movie industry is a close-knit one. Getting a job seems to be tied to knowing someone who has a job or knows about a job. The secret in finding the job you want often lies in taking an entry-level job that lets you make contacts in the industry and acquaints you with the different types of jobs available. Reading also helps. By reading *Variety* and *Hollywood Reporter*, two dailies about the movie business, you can find out what is happening in every phase of the industry, from new film stars to movies currently in production.

A Possible Starting Point

There is a rumor that Woody Allen started as a script typist. Whether this is true or not, the job is one that gives you a look at a lot of scripts. Being a script typist is excellent preparation for becoming a story analyst or a screenwriter. After you handle hundreds of scripts, you learn what is good and thoroughly understand the format in which scripts are written.

According to Valerie Koutnik, who was a script typist in Hollywood and is now a screenwriter, the job involves taking a script and putting it into the correct format. There are many complex rules for the layout of dialogue and descriptive passages, with different styles for film and television.

There are two basic requirements for getting a job as a script typist: you must be an excellent typist, and you must be a person who will safeguard the confidentiality of the scripts you type. Just think of how important script confidentiality is for the final television show of a season.

Valerie believes that a significant advantage of script-typing work is that it is one of the easier ways to get inside the film industry. Script typists can find work with independent production companies, studios, artists' agencies, freelance writers, and professional script-typing companies. You can find script-typing companies listed in the Los Angeles yellow pages.

Although the pay is hourly and the work can sometimes be tedious, Valerie feels it is invaluable experience in seeing how scripts are put together.

A Story Analyst

Working as a story analyst involves reading movie scripts, books, and plays to find one that has the potential to be made as a movie that will earn money. The whole industry is searching for these movies, so there are jobs at agencies, studios, production companies, and with individual stars. To work at most studios, you have to belong to a union. There are many places where you can read without belonging to a union, as well as many opportunities to be a freelancer. A freelancer can earn from $25 at the low end of the scale to $50 or more at the high end for reading each script. The pay range is from $60 to $200 or more for books and longer-than-usual scripts.

The Job Description. Story analysts read movie scripts, books, and plays and write coverages. Each studio, production company, or agency uses a different form for coverages, which involve the following three things:

1. A synopsis is written that retells the story as clearly as possible. The length and detail of the synopsis vary with the story analyst's employer.
2. The story analyst's opinion is given, explaining whether or not the story has commercial value, is castable, and is similar to other movies or well-known books.
3. A rating scale is usually filled in that rates such things as production value, structure, characterization, and dialogue on a scale from poor to excellent.

Job Qualifications. No degree is required for the job of story analyst. However, the analyst should have developed a literary sense from a lot of reading and a visual sense from having seen a lot of movies. Story analysts also need to know how to write.

One Bookworm's Job as a Story Analyst

With a degree in film, radio, and television in hand, Randy Kornfield entered the job market with the desire to become a screenwriter. A friend got him a part-time job duplicating scripts at a studio. Then he was promoted to the mail room. During this time he was meeting people and deciding where he wanted to work, as well as trying to write screenplays. A move to another studio brought Randy a job as a secretary and assistant in personnel. At this job, he met a story editor who let him read some scripts and write coverages. This gave him the chance to see what good and bad scripts were like, as well as what kinds of scripts were being bought. When this job folded, Randy became a freelance story analyst. Then he found a job at another studio as an assistant to an executive who was looking for scripts. At this job, which was primarily secretarial, he was able to read some scripts but didn't have to write coverages. After management changes at the studio, Randy was out of a job again. He next found a job as a story analyst at a nonunion studio. Then he was able to get a story analyst job at MGM, a union studio, because the story editor whom he met earlier was now working at this studio. This was followed by stints at 20th Century Fox and Sony Pictures. The advantage of working at a union studio is better pay plus benefits. Unfortunately, it is very difficult to get a job in a union studio.

During all this time, Randy was busy writing and has met with considerable success as a beginning screenwriter. You may have seen his holiday movie *Jingle All the Way*, starring Arnold Schwarzenegger, or the feature *Eight-Legged Freaks*. He has also written several movies that were produced on television. Reading scripts has been helpful in his writing. Plus, he receives considerable satisfaction in discovering scripts that have been turned into successful movies, such as *Talladega Nights* and *Superbad*.

Story Analyst for a Movie Star

Would you like to talk to a movie star on the phone or perhaps have him or her come to your office several times a week? All of this was part of Sandy Erickson's job as a story analyst when she read scripts and books looking for the right properties for Matt Dillon.

This was a glamour job that let Sandy read 70 percent of the time. You can find jobs like hers in the offices of managers and agents of movie stars.

Script Consultant

Many people dream of writing a successful movie or TV show and then becoming pals with all the Hollywood stars and directors. Unfortunately, more than 90 percent of all screenplay submissions never make it past a first read. For this reason, many work with a script consultant who has the expertise to analyze what they have written and give them feedback. You can live anywhere and be a script consultant. Depending on your expertise and the length of a script, you can earn from $70 to $200 for a complete evaluation. While this is definitely a reading job, you will also need to have some experience, such as being a writer or a story analyst. Or you can take a course in script consulting.

Fan Mail Reader

Movie stars get loads of letters from their fans. Almost all of this mail is handled by a fan club service provided by a star's manager, agent, or studio. Most of the letters are from people simply requesting pictures. The rest of the letters can usually be answered by form letters. Only a few letters require a personal reply.

A Production Company Executive

This is a glamorous job that let Matt Levy read 50 percent of the time while running Kiefer Sutherland's production company at 20th Century Fox. Matt spent much of his day searching for the right property for Kiefer to act in, produce, or direct. This involved reading a lot of scripts and books as well as newspapers and magazines for ideas. Matt also met with writers and listened to pitches—all to find possibilities for Kiefer's consideration.

Many actors have someone who reads for them because they don't have the time to evaluate all the materials out there when they are working. There are literally hundreds of ways to get these jobs—from starting in the mail room and building relations with people in the industry to working with an actor on a movie as Matt did with Kiefer. When you land a job like this, you may find yourself employed by a very eccentric actor, or you may be as lucky as Matt was and find yourself working for someone very pleasant. In any case, there is a lot of competition for these jobs.

Television—Almost Everyone's Favorite Medium

In both the United States and Canada, television sets are found in 99 percent of all homes. From the crack of dawn until late at night, the television set is rarely off in many households as people watch movies, quiz shows, soap operas, cartoons, educational programs, situation comedies, action-packed dramas, variety shows, news shows, or sports events. Overall, however, TV viewing in North America is down because people are devoting more time to using their computers. What is significant to the job seeker is that each show requires more people behind the scenes than the ones seen on the television screen. And many television jobs, both on camera and off, are good choices for bookworms who want jobs that require considerable reading.

A Network Story Editor

DeNece Gilbert knew that she wanted to work for a large television network even before she graduated from college with a communications degree. So, after graduation, she headed west—straight for Hollywood. Not knowing anyone and without any experience, she couldn't find a job in television. She did get a job in the publishing division of Motown Records, which required her to place songs with the appropriate Motown artists.

After gaining experience at Motown, DeNece became a secretary at a major television network. Several promotions later, she was the assistant to the director of comedy and drama. This job was a bookworm's delight. DeNece read scripts and treatments and wrote a one-page synopsis of each work for the director. She worked on the weekly episodes of many popular shows.

Today, DeNece is working for a major network in New York City as a story editor covering books. It is her job to find books that would make good television movies or miniseries. She works with thirty large publishing houses in New York and thirty other smaller publishing houses throughout the country. Her only job is to look for good stories. DeNece does not do any writing or rewriting. The network hires writers or uses in-house writers for any changes or adaptations that are needed.

On the job, most of DeNece's reading time is spent going through publishing catalogs. She usually orders ten or eleven books from each catalog. DeNece also looks through *Kirkus Reviews*, which lists upcoming books, and *Publishers Weekly*. She reads popular consumer magazines as well as newspapers to discover future trends. She usually takes manuscripts and books home to read so that she can read them without interruption.

DeNece can't read everything, so she has ten freelance readers who keep busy reading for her. They write a two-and-a-half-page summary of each book, plus a one-page personal comment sheet. If a freelancer suggests a second reading or praises the work, DeNece reads the material. It takes more than one year from the time material goes into development until it is seen on the air. DeNece looks for fresh work and often chooses first-time authors.

Glamour does enter into this ideal job for a bookworm. The casting office is right next to DeNece's office. There are trips to large book fairs and the Louisville Playwright's Festival. At this festival, she is not only looking at the plays but is also on the lookout for good new writers.

According to DeNece, networks have many other jobs that bookworms would like. Script readers are needed for every division in a network. For the children's after-school specials, the readers even read children's books to find new program ideas. There are also jobs for research librarians.

Talk-Show Producer

All those talk shows you see on television have producers. Some even have producers for each segment of the show. These producers are responsible for what happens on a show—a job usually requiring considerable reading.

A talk-show producer may read the books of authors who are going to be on the program and then frame questions for the show's host. Then there are all the books that land on the talk-show producer's desk; these must be looked at to see which authors should be selected to appear on the program. Research may also be done on each guest on the program to acquaint the host with the day's guest or guests. Furthermore, there is the task of keeping up with what is happening in the world so provocative guests and subjects can be chosen. A daily talk show consumes a lot of material, so the search for new ideas is never ending. Most of these ideas evolve from the reading done by the show's producer or producers.

Jobs as producers and segment producers are not usually entry-level jobs, except at smaller television stations. To be a producer of a major network show requires previous experience. A producer might start at a station as an assistant, advance to associate producer, and then be a coordinating producer before becoming a producer.

A News-Show Producer

Producers of TV talk shows aren't the only ones who read. News-show producers also must read. Mike Weir was the producer for a late-afternoon half-hour show for a major station in San Francisco. The show dealt mainly with local and national news of the day. After the top news stories aired, the stories geared toward medicine, women, children, consumer issues, and other topics appropriate for the time slot's audience.

Producers like Mike read all day long to keep themselves constantly updated on what is happening in the world. He needed this knowledge because he decided the editorial content of this news show in collaboration with the producers of other news shows. Mike was also busy determining the order in which stories were presented on the show, the look of the show, the graphics used, the use of live shots, and the myriad details that guarantee a smooth production.

Producing a news show is not just reading. Mike did loads of writing for the program. Writing for television is quite different from writing for other media. The language must be simple, and so must the sentences. On his show, the writing had to be for the ear because many people at this time in the afternoon watch TV while doing other things.

Mike started working in television as the weekend producer of a news show in a small market. He was able to do this because he attended a college that had a broadcasting program that allowed him to get experience producing shows while he was still in school. Mike has now climbed the career ladder to be the executive producer at a different channel.

A News Anchor on a Midwest Station

Maybe some news anchors are just performers. However, Tom Cochrun, former evening news anchor at an NBC station in Indianapolis, was not one of them. Tom is a true bookworm who, as a child, stayed up many evenings with a flashlight trying to finish the sports adventure books that got him hooked on reading.

In his job as news anchor, Tom read for 60 to 80 percent of his workday. He read newspapers, research reports, background reports, and magazines. Tom felt that in order to write news copy that his viewers would understand, he needed a strong grasp of the information. He says he could not get this understanding from just reading wire-service information. Most of the big stars of network news do a great deal of reading to prepare for their shows.

Public Relations

Companies, institutions, unions, activist groups, and all kinds of organizations want to win public approval. The people who help them win this approval are in the public relations field, which is commonly called PR. Some organizations have their own public relations departments, while others use public relations firms. In either case, the task is to communicate with a specific audience. Airlines may want to stress how safe it is to fly after several crashes have shaken the public's confidence in air travel. A chemical company may want to reassure its workers on the safety of the workplace. A food company may want to communicate to its stockholders the reasons why the price of its stock is steadily falling.

People employed in public relations work have two main activities: research and communication. Most of the glamour lies in the communication side because PR people arrange for media publicity. It is the research side that allows bookworms to read. In order to handle an account, it is essential to be well versed in what a client does. This may mean reading not only about a company, but also about an entire industry. The majority of reading is probably done to find out what newspapers and magazines are writing about their clients. It is also important to gather information that may affect a client. Today's public relations employees are voracious readers who must read everything in order to serve their clients effectively.

Travel Agent

The type of reading that travel agents do is frequently investigative. Cynthia Kroos, the managing director of a travel agency, finds it essential to learn about new tourist spots, resorts, and tours. She is constantly reading trade publications to do this. Obviously, a lot of reading also has to be done to keep up with all the packages that are offered by airlines and tour companies. According to Cynthia, travel agents have so much reading to do that it can almost bury them. Because so much of the workday is devoted to dealing with clients, considerable reading must be done at home. The glamorous bonus to all of this reading is the frequent trips that Cynthia takes to learn more about places her clients may wish to visit.

Reading Can Be Glamorous

While a glamour career may be appealing to many people, including bookworms, it is not easy to break into a glamorous field. Even college graduates are usually required to begin in low-level positions because experience is needed for the positions they seek. Few have that experience, so graduates are often forced to begin as secretaries, typists, or gofers to gain experience. There is always room for good people in glamour industries. However, getting the job of your dreams involves hard work as well as luck, perseverance, and good timing.

Glamour careers at all levels can be pressure filled and tension packed as people struggle to meet deadlines for such things as television shows, advertising promotions, and movie productions. There is no guarantee of a nine-to-five job. Like all careers, considerable drudgery is involved. However, glamour careers do offer involvement in exciting industries such as radio, television, the movies, public relations, and travel, which makes these careers so sought after.

For Further Reading

The more you know about the glamour industries, the easier it will be for you to discover the job you want. A surprising number of jobs in this industry are filled by people who read for a substantial period of time each day. While most bookworms are working behind the scenes in these industries, a few are also in the public eye. The following books should give you a better idea of what careers are available in the glamour industries.

Broady, Jack. *On-Air: The Guidebook to Starting a Career as a Radio Personality*. Riverside, CA: BVI Books, 2007.

Careers in Advertising and Public Relations. San Francisco: WetFeet, Inc., 2006.

Careers in Focus: Public Relations. New York: Ferguson Publishing Company, 2007.

Mitchell, Gerald E. *Global Travel and Tourism Career Opportunities*. Charleston, SC: The Gem Group, Ltd., 2006.

Schneider, Chris. *Starting Your Career in Broadcasting: Working On and Off the Air in Radio and Television*. New York: Allworth Press, 2007.

Taylor, Allan, James Robert Parrish, and Nat Segaloff. *Career Opportunities in Television and Cable*, 2nd ed. New York: Checkmark Books, 2006.

CHAPTER SEVEN

Education Careers
Helping Others Learn

eaching is a powerful job—you can never tell where your influence stops. You have the opportunity to transmit your love of books to your students and create a new generation of bookworms. And being a teacher also lets you work closely with books, for successful teachers love books, read books, and understand them. Nevertheless, being a bookworm is not enough to make someone a good teacher. Good teachers must also be able to pass the knowledge, skills, and information that they have acquired from books on to their students. It is appropriate that teaching is the largest profession in the world. If there were no teachers, people would have to learn so much on their own, and so much of the knowledge that has been accumulated from past generations would disappear. It is as teacher-astronaut Christa McAuliffe said, "I touch the future. I teach."

Preparing to Teach

Teaching is not a new profession. Scholars like Aristotle, Plato, and Socrates were teachers. But it was not until the 1800s that teaching schools began to develop. Today, anyone planning to teach, whether in a kindergarten or at the college or university level, needs a college degree. Many elementary, middle school, junior high, and high school teachers also need to get master's degrees to advance in the profession and to increase earnings. Bookworms who want to teach at the college level often need doctorates. Prospective elementary, middle school, junior high, and senior high school teachers study similar courses during their first two years of college. These are basic liberal arts courses and include the study of history, language arts, mathematics, and science. During their college years, they also take teaching methods courses and do actual practice teaching in a classroom under the guidance of an experienced teacher. In addition, future high school teachers and many middle school and junior high teachers specialize in the particular subject areas in which they plan to teach.

Before most bookworms can start teaching, they need to meet state and provincial requirements for teacher certification. These requirements deal with the college courses that teachers must complete satisfactorily to become certified as elementary, middle school, junior high, and senior high school teachers in public schools. Each state and Canadian province has different requirements. In some states and provinces, teachers at nursery schools, private schools, and community colleges also have to be certified. However, teachers at four-year colleges and universities do not need state or provincial certification.

General Teaching Duties

All teachers, no matter what level they are teaching, have a number of duties that must be performed—from taking attendance to filling out report cards.

Getting Ready. Bookworms find classroom preparation enjoyable because it involves so much reading. Teachers read textbooks, teacher's manuals, course-related materials, professional journals, and curriculum guides and visit websites to prepare for their daily stint in the classroom. However, preparation goes beyond reading to making sure everything is completely ready for each lesson. Materials must be duplicated, and supplementary books and materials as well as supplies must be obtained and laid out in readiness for each class.

Leading the Way. Teachers are the classroom leaders. Through a variety of teaching methods, they motivate their students to learn, show them how to learn, and instill intellectual curiosity in them. Books help teachers in this task, as do all kinds of audio-visual materials, such as CDs, tapes, filmstrips, videos, movies, and television programs, plus all the things that can be done with computers.

Checking Progress. All teachers need to make sure that their students have learned the material. Mastery is important, whether it is the alphabet, the multiplication tables, or French grammar. Teachers check their students' progress through analyzing written and oral work, quizzes, and tests. Records need to be kept, increasingly on computers, so that teachers know how each individual student is doing. This information must be placed on report cards and discussed at conferences with parents.

Being a Role Model. Students do notice how their teachers behave. Younger students, especially, often want to be just like their teachers. Teachers set a very powerful example for their students through their own sincerity, patience, kindness, understanding, honesty, and objectivity. Furthermore, teachers who truly love to read inspire their students to become lifelong readers, and a new generation of bookworms emerges.

Doing the Extra Tasks. Teachers have other obligations besides routine classroom tasks. They are also expected to take a share of duties, such as hall and playground duty and supervising the lunchroom and bus loading. They chaperone many after-school events, attend faculty meetings, and sponsor clubs. You should not consider teaching as a profession if you expect to be home by 3 P.M. each day.

Teaching at the Lower Elementary Level

For bookworms, teaching children in the lower elementary grades can be very satisfying. These teachers have the opportunity to actually teach young children how to read and to help each child develop an appreciation for books. It is a chance for bookworms to instill their love of books in others.

According to Fran Hageboeck, a first grade teacher for many years, half of her teaching day is devoted to some aspect of teaching reading. During that time, she reads out loud to the class for thirty minutes. She also spends time having children read to her and listening as they read to each other. Away from the classroom, she spends time in the library searching for books to read to the children and for them to read. Of course, first grade teachers teach subjects besides reading. They also spend time tying shoes, buttoning coats, putting on boots, and handing out tissues. But reading is the main focus of all the learning activities in first grade.

Teaching at the Upper Elementary or Middle School Level

If you were turned off by the need to tie shoes and button coats at the lower elementary level but still like children, you might find it more enjoyable to teach in one of the upper elementary grades or in middle school. In fourth, fifth, and sixth grades, students can handle all their own personal needs and have also mastered the basic reading skills. Teachers at these grade levels are helping students become independent learners. Besides classes in reading and mathematics, students are now beginning to learn in the content areas of history, science, health, and English. For bookworms, it is an opportunity to help children expand their horizons through a broad reading program.

The trend today is to teach thematic units in which students study a topic such as California and learn about its history, geography, and geology throughout the day as they study social studies, language arts, science, and mathematics. Searching for materials to use in this approach has Karen McCall, a fourth grade teacher, reading avidly. Then, to keep up with what is happening in her profession, she reads newsletters and professional journals. Finally, she reads local papers and periodicals to keep abreast of community happenings. For Karen, reading plays an important role in the quality of instruction she brings to the classroom.

Teaching at the Junior High Level

Sue Engledow, a true bookworm, made a career change from being a bank manager to being a junior high school science teacher. Sue decided that she wanted to spend more time with books than with numbers. She went back to college and took the required education courses. Due to the influence of an elementary science teacher, Sue decided to become a science teacher. Sue has been teaching science to seventh graders in a suburban junior high school for more than ten years.

Sue finds that science teachers do considerable reading. She usually has one concentrated preparation period each week. During this time, she reads for three to four hours. Besides reading the teacher's manual, she reads the student textbook, then she takes notes and makes outlines for herself and her students. Arriving an hour early every morning gives Sue the time to read over all her notes and outlines for the day, along with reading and preparing for the laboratory work her students will be doing.

Sue's reading time is not just devoted to preparation for her classes. She prepares all her own tests, so she has to spend more hours rereading all the material to develop these tests. If she gives an essay test, she has to spend additional hours reading the students' papers. Sue reads for another two to three hours every evening so that she is able to enhance what her students are reading in their textbooks.

Teaching at the High School Level

Giving students objectives before each reading assignment is Felice Knarr's way of developing critical readers in her twelfth grade English literature classes. Felice has been teaching English at a private high school for several years.

In August, before school starts, Felice charts her course of study for the entire school year. She reads every book that the students will be reading so that she knows how long each reading assignment should take.

This is not the only time Felice reads the material that will be assigned to her students. Before each reading assignment is made, she rereads the material to develop the objectives for her lesson plans. Beyond all the reading that Felice does in her preparation, she also spends six to eight hours a week grading the essays and compositions of her one hundred students. This does not include the reading that she must do in grading vocabulary, spelling, and short writing assignments.

Felice is a true bookworm who always seems to be reading. She spends several hours each day reading academic journals. It is common for her to spend eight to twelve hours on weekends keeping up with her academic reading because she is taking courses to complete her master's degree in English. For relaxation, Felice likes to read magazines.

Teaching at the College Level

The usual entry-level teaching position at the college level is as an instructor or assistant professor. Then the battle commences to get tenure, which is permanent faculty status. During the trial years before tenure is granted, which ranges from seven to ten years, assistant professors struggle to make names for themselves. The usual method at universities is by publishing papers for journals and books. This is the reason for the expression "publish or perish."

During this probationary period, reading fills every spare minute of an assistant professor's time, as research is done to produce the needed publications. The reading at this stage must necessarily be quite narrow within the teaching field. After the desired tenure is granted, reading can become much broader so that a fuller understanding of a particular field of study is achieved.

Assistant professors eventually become associate and then full professors, and some even become department chairpersons. Reading is an absolute necessity throughout an academic career. Teachers at the college level must keep up with what is happening in their individual fields and must read to develop new courses.

Teaching in Special Programs

There are many other teachers besides classroom teachers. Today, most elementary and middle schools have reading, speech, music, and physical education teachers on their teaching staffs. These teachers have specialized in a particular subject area, just as teachers in junior and senior high schools do. There are also teachers who work in gifted and talented programs and in special education. Some teachers become counselors, curriculum directors, and principals.

Other Positions in Education

Bookworms who are interested in education but don't want to work in the classroom can find satisfying jobs besides teaching that involve reading.

College Admissions Counselor

According to Steve Bushouse, former dean of admissions at Butler University in Indianapolis, you need strong basic reading skills to work as an admissions counselor at a college. However, he points out that you need other skills, too, in order to be successful at this job. Counselors in the admissions office need to be very people oriented. Not only do admissions counselors interview students, they also give speeches at schools and work in booths at college fairs.

College admissions counselors read and evaluate high school records. Then, as part of a committee, they decide which students will be admitted to the college. In this job, entire days—often far into the night—are spent reading. Furthermore, this is not a five-day-a-week job, especially when applications are being read.

Curriculum Director

Within most large school districts, there are jobs for curriculum directors. Some may be in charge of an area such as elementary or high school curricula, while others direct the curriculum of a single subject area, such as reading, mathematics, or science. In any case, this is one job that involves a great deal of reading as new textbooks are selected and new curriculums are developed. Jobs in curriculum planning should also interest bookworms.

Reading Consultant

The Department of Education in each state and province has advisory positions that would appeal to bookworms. One position that involves reading is working as a reading consultant. These consultants need to read widely so that they can advise teachers on the wide variety of materials that can be used in the classroom.

Education Association Professional

In the United States, there are many professional organizations for teachers. More than half of all teachers belong to either the

National Education Association (NEA) or the American Federation of Teachers (AFT). These organizations bargain with school systems over wages, hours, and other terms and conditions of employment. Canadian teachers belong to either provincial or territorial associations that are concerned with working conditions as well as professional development. There are also professional associations for administrators, such as the National Association of Secondary School Principals in the United States and the Canadian Association of Principals in Canada. All of the education organizations and associations offer jobs for bookworms in different capacities, ranging from researching to copyediting.

Travel Opportunities for Teachers

If you are a bookworm who likes to travel, there are many teaching jobs in all parts of the world. The pay is not always as good as it is in the United States or Canada, but the opportunities for travel and adventure are often an added pull for bookworms looking for excitement. If you are interested in working abroad as a teacher, you can use a search engine to look for jobs online, and you can visit the websites of the organizations listed here.

UNITED STATES TEACHERS
Fulbright Teacher Exchange Program
www.fulbrightexchanges.org

Department of Defense Education Activity
www.dodea.edu

Peace Corps
www.peacecorps.gov

CANADIAN TEACHERS
www.teachingoverseas.ca

Teacher Salaries

Teacher salaries are constantly increasing, although they vary greatly among states and provinces. They typically increase each year based on cost-of-living increases, merit, years of experience, and educational degrees. In the United States, the average annual earnings of teachers range from $43,000 to $48,000. Those with the lowest salaries earn between $28,000 and $33,000 while those with the highest salaries earn between $67,000 and $76,000.

Depending on where you teach in Canada, the average salary for those with four years of education varies from a minimum of a little more than CAN$30,000 to a maximum of CAN$62,000. Teachers with six years of education earn between a minimum of CAN$38,000 and a maximum of CAN$73,000.

If you are interested in knowing the starting salaries for schools in your area, you can get this information from your state or provincial Department of Education or your local school district. Teachers can boost their salaries in a number of ways, from coaching sports to working with students in extracurricular activities.

The salaries of college teachers vary with the rank and type of institution, geographic area, and field. Many faculty members have significant earnings in addition to their base salary, from consulting, teaching additional courses, doing research, and writing for publication.

By rank, the average salary for full professors in the United States was $98,974 in 2006, with $69,911 for associate professors, $58,662 for assistant professors, $42,609 for instructors, and $48,289 for lecturers. In Canada, senior university professors earned between CAN$60,500 and CAN$111,5000 in 2004.

The Job Outlook for Teachers

Today, education is the largest profession in North America. There are more than six million teachers in the United States and more than three hundred thousand in Canada. Half of the teachers in the United States are elementary and middle school teachers, while 80 percent of the Canadian teachers have jobs below the secondary level.

Overall, job opportunities for teachers in the United States through 2016 will vary from good to excellent depending on where you teach, the grade level, and the subject taught. There is considerable demand for qualified teachers to teach science (especially chemistry), bilingual education, foreign languages, and vocational education. In Canada, the opportunities for teaching jobs at all levels are only fair through 2010.

For Further Reading

Teaching is a bookworm's career today more than ever. The responsibilities and workloads of teachers have increased along with the volume of reading that must be done in order to keep pace with the rapid accumulation of knowledge.

The following books provide a good look at getting a job in the teaching profession.

Babb, Danielle, and Jim Mirabella. *Make Money Teaching Online: How to Land Your First Academic Job, Build Credibility, and Earn a Six-Figure Salary.* Hoboken, NJ: Wiley, 2007.

Clement, Mary C. *The Definitive Guide to Getting a Teaching Job: An Insider's Guide to Finding the Right Job, Writing the Perfect Resume, and Nailing the Interview.* Lanham, MD: Rowman & Littlefield Education, 2007.

Echaore-McDavid, Susan. *Career Opportunities in Education and Related Services,* 2nd ed. New York: Checkmark Books, 2006.

Enelow, Wendy S., and Louise M. Kursmark. *Expert Resumes for Teachers and Educators.* Indianapolis, IN: JIST Works, 2005.

Feirsen, Robert, and Seth Wietzman. *How to Get the Teaching Job You Want: The Complete Guide for College Graduates, Returning Teachers and Career Changers*, 2nd ed. Sterling, VA: Stylus Publishing, 2004.

Warner, Jack, Clyde Bryan, and Diane Warner. *Inside Secrets of Finding a Teaching Job*, 3rd ed. Indianapolis, IN: JIST Works, 2006.

CHAPTER EIGHT

Research Careers

Finding and Assembling Information

For how many days in a year is there a likelihood of a hurricane striking an island in the Caribbean or the city of New Orleans? Who is the current leader of the opposition party in Germany? Where is the oldest operating nuclear plant in the world located? Which country in Asia has the highest number of people under the age of ten? What are the latest figures on car sales in Kuwait?

Governments, businesses, and individuals often need questions like these answered in order to make important decisions. For challenging questions, they often turn to researchers who know exactly where to look for difficult-to-find answers. Plus, researchers often dig for information so that papers, books, and reports can be written. While doing research is definitely not a large job area, it is one that is steadily growing because of the importance of research in making so many significant decisions in today's very complicated world.

Being a researcher is definitely a great job for bookworms as it may let you read all day on the job. In addition to reading books, periodicals, and other documents, most of today's researchers do a considerable amount of work on the Internet. If you are curious and would like to know more about any subject in the world, from the environment to the latest medical discoveries to ancient history, a career in research may be right for you. You'll find these jobs at universities; think tanks; local, state or provincial, and federal government units; museums; historic sites; publishers; and even zoos. You can even be a self-employed information search specialist.

Research Jobs at Universities

Universities are true research centers. A large university has numerous research projects going on all the time. Jobs become available whenever a new project is started. Many university projects are headed by resident faculty members; others are led by accomplished scholars from other universities who have come to the university to work on a research project. To head a project, you must have outstanding credentials. A doctorate degree is the basic requirement. Then you have to demonstrate that you are an expert in your field.

Fortunately for those who want to be researchers at a university, research projects need to have more staff people than the one person heading the project. In some cases, the lead researcher may only work at it part-time on the project, leaving a lot of work for staff researchers. Although people seeking research staff positions don't need the same professional status as the project heads, they do need top-notch qualifications to land these desirable jobs. The competition for jobs as entry-level research assistants can be so intense at prestigious universities that you could be competing against fifty or more applicants.

Research Assistant

There are different levels of research assistants. To climb each rung on the ladder, or to start beyond an entry-level position, you need more than a bachelor's degree, plus experience. You also have to demonstrate that you can evaluate and analyze what you read. As you move to higher levels, your responsibilities increase. You may become responsible for a phase of a project or an entire project.

You can learn about entry-level jobs in research through university employment offices, bulletins, and websites. These jobs do not require as much reading as bookworms would probably like. Usually, you can expect to spend about half of your time extracting information—that's the reading portion of the job—and the other half doing clerical work. In fact, having some clerical experience and knowing how to use a computer are prerequisites for getting entry-level jobs.

As a research assistant, you usually only work on one project at a time. This does give you the opportunity to become an expert on a subject through your reading. Some projects have a time limit, while others go on as more funding becomes available. After one project is finished, researchers typically go on to work on another project.

Research Jobs at Think Tanks

If you are constantly reading newspapers and newsmagazines to keep up with what is going on in the world and would like to do this for a living, then a job at a think tank could be ideal for you. Think tanks are a twentieth-century phenomenon made up of groups of researchers who seek and analyze information for governmental units, special-interest groups, businesses, and the public. This information is primarily used by government policy makers and bureaucrats to make decisions on policies. A researcher at a think tank could have a role in influencing legislation on the proper amount of financial aid for a Southeast Asian country or environmental controls on mining operations.

When you hear the words *think tank*, you may conjure visions of intellectuals concentrating on heady problems. It is decidedly true that considerable thinking goes on at think tanks, but much of that thinking is based upon reading and research. Until the 1970s, there were no more than several dozen think tanks in North America. Today, there are at least two thousand, representing a wide range of the political spectrum. There are also government think tanks, especially in the area of defense and security. Many of today's think tanks are far more activist than the earlier ones. While still producing books and papers, think tanks now actively lobby legislators and court the press to influence the government. So, besides researching and writing, the think tank employee's job description has to be rewritten to include public relations work.

The first generation of think tanks was slightly to the left or right of center in political thinking. However, research tended to show both viewpoints. Following the volatile 1960s, specialized think tanks that considered only one issue began to evolve. Many of today's think tanks have strong conservative or liberal roots; however, some of the newer think tanks are taking more objective views. A new trend, resulting from globalization, has think tanks throughout the world collaborating with each other. Nevertheless, people thinking of applying for a job at a think tank should probably consider their own political biases when deciding where to look for a job. Here is a list of some of the prominent think tanks in the United States and Canada:

UNITED STATES
American Enterprise Institute
Brookings Institution
Cato Institute
Center for American Progress
Center for Defense Information
Center for National Policy
Claremont Institute
Heritage Foundation
Hoover Institution
Hudson Institute
Institute for Policy Studies

RAND Corporation
Tellus Institute

CANADA
Caledon Institute of Social Policy
Canadian Institute of International Affairs
C.D. Howe Institute
Fraser Institute
Institute for Research on Public Policy

There are a few state and province-based think tanks in the United States and Canada; however, the majority are concerned with national issues. Traditionally, most think tanks are located close to Washington, D.C., or New York City in the United States and Ottawa and Toronto in Canada, although there are exceptions. One of the earliest conservative think tanks, the Hoover Institution, which was founded in 1919, is located in California. The Hudson Institute really overturned the East Coast emphasis by moving from a location near New York City to Indianapolis, Indiana, in 1984, although the headquarters were moved to Washington, D.C., in 2004.

Working at a Think Tank

You may bump into many people who were formerly in the political limelight if you have a think tank job. Former secretaries of state Henry Kissinger, George Schultz, and Madeleine Albright; President Jimmy Carter and his national security advisor Zbigniew Brzezinski; and Mikhail Gorbachev are now or have been associated in the past with think tanks. Of course, most of the people working at think tanks don't have names that you see every day in the newspaper. But many are quite well-known scholars in their fields of expertise or show promise of being future academic superstars. At the older think tanks, you are more likely to work with well-known scholars and people who have made their names in government. The stars at the newer think tanks tend to be political activists instead of former government officials.

First-Level Researcher

If your vision of the perfect job is one where your desk is inundated with reading materials, an entry-level job at a think tank may be the right one for you. To get this type of job, impressive credentials are needed. For most jobs, some type of graduate degree—usually a master's degree—is essential. You also need some experience in doing research, even if it is only writing your own research papers. When seeking a job, it can be helpful to know someone involved in a project at a think tank in order to discover what jobs are available; however, sending out resumes is also a good way to get a job.

If you have a job as a first-level researcher, you can work on researching just one topic for a think tank scholar or on a number of topics for different people. When a project starts, you will read to get a basic understanding of an issue. Then you may be asked to develop a bibliography for the head of the project. At times, you will summarize what you read. You may even be given a particular issue on which to focus. You will have considerable autonomy in deciding how your job will be performed. Ultimately, scholars at the think tank write papers or books on the topics that have been researched.

To advance up the ladder from a first-level researcher, a doctorate is usually required. To get a feel for what a job is like at a think tank, you should consider taking an internship at one of these institutions.

Archivists

Not too many people are acquainted with what archives are or what archivists do. First of all, archives are records of individuals, groups, institutions, and governments at all levels that are preserved because they have information of lasting value. Such historic documents as the Declaration of Independence, the U.S. Constitution, and the Bill of Rights are preserved in the National Archives in Washington, D.C. Canadian historic documents are preserved in the Library and Archives Canada. All of the valuable documents from each president's term of office in the United States are preserved in presidential libraries, which are archives. You can also find the records that must be kept by law for local and state and provincial governments in archives. Archival records are not just government documents. Businesses have archives; so do universities, hospitals, labor unions, and even small historical societies.

Records may be saved on any medium, including paper, film, videotape, audiotape, or electronic data. They also may be copied onto some other format to protect the original and make them more accessible to researchers who use the records.

The Job of an Archivist

The primary job of an archivist is to establish control over records. This involves organizing records so they can easily be accessed. A collection must have a title, and all of the contents must be organized in a logical sequence and described so they can be used. The job also requires a judgment of what records have historical value; for example, the federal government of the United States saves only 3 percent of its records. Much of the work of the archivist, therefore, is going through documents to decide which should be kept permanently. All of these tasks require reading. Not only must the documents be read, the archivist needs to understand the historical period in which they were created to understand their value.

Another job of the archivist is overseeing the preservation of documents. Because original newsprint will not last, the archivist must supervise the reproduction of newspaper clippings onto acid-free paper. Archivists must also determine whether to try to restore an original document that has been damaged or conserve it by microfilming it. The preservation work is done by scientific and technical specialists.

The archivist's job also includes gathering information that is requested. Archivists are becoming more involved, too, in the publication and exhibition of materials. In addition, some archivists have the task of soliciting funds to preserve or establish a collection. And, of course, archivists who are in charge of collections have administrative responsibilities involved in supervising a staff.

What you earn as an archivist varies with where you work and live. Generally, the larger or better-funded institutions offer larger salaries. The average annual earnings of archivists in the United States are approximately $40,000, while those in Canada are CAN$56,000.

Requirements for Becoming an Archivist

The one personal characteristic that archivists have in common, no matter where they work, is an interest in preserving the past. There is also a need for organizational ability, good judgment, an interest in research, and self-reliance.

While there may be some entry-level jobs that require only a bachelor's degree, a master's degree is much more common. Undergraduate majors can vary, but master's degrees are usually in either history or library science. Increasingly, job candidates have master's degrees in both areas, with course work in the theory and practice of archives. Currently, there are very few college programs offering bachelor's or master's degrees in archival science. For senior staff positions, especially at universities, a doctorate may be required.

Once a person decides to be an archivist, it is usually a lifetime career. At first, archivists may move from one archive to another, but most eventually stay in one place. And that place may well be a governmental unit because the majority of archivists have civil service standing. Those who work at universities may also be faculty members.

The archival profession is a growing one. One way to learn more about this profession is by contacting the Society of American Archivists (www.archivists.org) in the United States and the Association of Canadian Archivists (www.archivists.ca).

. . . .

Curators

Like archivists, curators are concerned with keeping records of the past. The difference is that archivists are primarily concerned with written materials, while curators are primarily concerned with objects and specimens. You will find curators at museums, zoos, aquariums, botanical gardens, and historic sites. Curators who work for the federal government in the United States are found in the Smithsonian Institution, military museums, and archaeological and other museums run by the Department of the Interior. Most curator jobs in Canada are found in federal and provincial museums.

The Curator's Job

A curator's job varies depending on the size of the institution. In a small institution, the curator must not only acquire, identify, catalog, and store objects, but also perform restoration work, arrange for exhibitions, and conduct educational programs. This job description can be further expanded to include doing all the research and the hammering and nailing when it comes to setting up an exhibition. At a large institution, a curator might specialize in a particular area—such as toys, anthropology, science, or technology—or be assigned a function—such as cataloging, acquisitions, or restoration.

Whether a curator has a specific responsibility or is responsible for everything at an institution, considerable reading is essential in this job. When an institution acquires new objects or specimens, curators must read to identify them accurately. When a new exhibit is being set up, the curator researches to see what belongs in the exhibit and that everything is properly displayed. Curators must also read to learn about the newest and best ways to preserve and display objects and specimens. There is also reading to answer questions posed by the public. And, of course, considerable reading of professional journals is essential to keep up with what is happening in the profession.

Requirements for Becoming a Curator

While some curators have earned bachelor's or master's degrees in museum studies (museology), many institutions are looking for curators with degrees in specific areas, such as art, anthropology, biology, or history.

The minimum requirements for obtaining a curator's job are a bachelor's degree and experience. Most museums, however, want curators to have a master's degree in a specific field plus experience. Curators working in smaller institutions may also need some business courses to handle administrative responsibilities.

There are fewer than thirty thousand jobs for archivists and curators in North America, but because of the current interest in art, history, technology, and culture, the number of curators is growing. However, there will never be a great number of openings for jobs as curators. Furthermore, the job is appealing to many qualified applicants, so there is considerable competition. Those who have had experience as interns or volunteers often have the best chance to get these coveted jobs. Curators' salaries are similar to those of archivists.

Historians

Why did Winston Churchill lose his post as prime minister after successfully leading Britain through World War II? How successful was the first Five-Year Plan in China in terms of stimulating agricultural production? Historians formulate questions like these to direct their studies of the past. They are imaginative researchers who read all kinds of documents to determine what happened in the past, why it happened, and how it has affected the present and may affect the future. After collecting data by reading vast amounts of material, historians analyze the information and then present it in the form of textbooks, lectures, studies, reports, and articles.

Most historians—more than 70 percent of them—are college or university teachers who conduct research and write as well as carry out their teaching duties. The remaining historians work at jobs where their historical skills and knowledge are required. This may mean writing histories for companies and governmental units. It can mean researching historical records for businesses, law firms, television or movie companies, and public agencies. It can also mean analyzing past trends for banks, insurance companies, investment services, manufacturers, utilities, and public relations firms. No matter where a historian works, the job is ideal for bookworms because it always allows them to read while doing their jobs.

Education and Job Opportunities

Because most historians work as college teachers, a doctorate in history is almost essential to obtain employment. Teaching jobs open up when faculty members retire or enrollment in history courses increases.

Opportunities to obtain a position as a historian are quite limited. Overall, fewer than one thousand job openings for historians occur each year. There is keen competition for these openings, whether they are at colleges, museums, archives, historical societies, businesses, or with the government. Only a few historians are self-employed as writers, consultants, or researchers.

A Historian in Women's Studies

Until recently, the role of women has been overlooked in history. There was a dearth of material written on this subject. Sara Evans, a University of Minnesota professor, is a historian who recognized that the history of women was undervalued. Hired by the university to teach women's history, Sara combined this job with the writing of scholarly works on women. Her approach is not to romanticize the role of women by telling of heroines but to prove that women whose names aren't household words have helped to shape the United States.

Sara's research has taken her to libraries, museums, and archives to answer questions about the past. An important part of her research has been figuring out what type of material to study. For example, to find out about the diet and workload of slaves, her students have studied plantation records.

Both Sara's teaching duties and research in women's studies have entailed considerable reading. Obviously, historians are readers; however, the time Sara spends reading varies enormously. When she is on leave, she reads as much as forty hours a week. The pluses to her work are that she feels she is doing something new all the time and that her work is making a difference in the way people see the past.

Researchers for Publishers

When you read an article in an encyclopedia, the *New Yorker*, *National Geographic*, *Newsweek*, or *Time*, you expect the facts to be accurate. There is a small brigade of workers at these organizations who research to make sure that the facts you read are accurate. They are seekers of the truth, whether their job titles are fact-checkers, junior researchers, or senior researchers. These researchers spend their days reading and phoning as they go over articles word by word to make them reliable.

The backgrounds of these researchers vary. However, a knowledge of research techniques and an insatiable desire to find the facts are essential. It is also necessary to be able to write clearly because these researchers must explain proposed changes.

Researching for an Encyclopedia Publisher

As a child, Cheryl Graham would read Nancy Drew books and dream of being a detective. Today, as chief researcher of special projects for World Book, she fulfills that dream as she acts as a sleuth, digging up hard-to-find facts for the encyclopedia and other publications. Being a fact detective involves using the computer to research current information. Online, Cheryl visits many different websites, including those of newspapers, newswires, governmental bodies, and universities. When looking up historical information, she is more apt to use printed sources and may visit special libraries. Half of Cheryl's time is spent researching major encyclopedia articles on topics such as individual countries, drug abuse, and evolution. The rest of her time is spent checking the facts of articles submitted by contributors for special World Book publications. For example, it may take her a day to check the facts on a biographical sketch of Frank Gehry, the famous architect who designed the art museum in Bilbao, Spain. A lengthy article on environmental pollution, however, could require as long as a month to check the facts thoroughly because it involves talking with experts and finding many different sources.

All of Cheryl's jobs have involved considerable reading. At her first job with the Library of Congress, she set up a library for congressional staffers doing research on environmental policy. This meant sitting down and reading articles like crazy so she could abstract and index them. She then worked at two other libraries as a reference librarian before coming to World Book.

This bookworm never tires of looking up interesting facts and reading about them. Cheryl's job as a researcher has become more interesting as the breadth of her knowledge increases. Her on-the-job reading has lead her to latch onto subjects and pursue them further in her free time. As a result, she has become an expert in several topics, including historical textiles.

Information Brokers

When businesses, organizations, and even individuals need specific information to solve problems or answer questions, they call on information brokers. Being an information broker is essentially being a researcher. It is also being a reader because brokers use libraries and online databases to find specific information for their clients. Some brokers specialize in a particular area, such as the environment, biotechnology, or patents. Careers in information brokering have really just emerged in the past thirty years. Choose a career in this area, and you will probably work alone; there are few information-brokering companies. And each job will bring a new challenge to find information, so you will never be bored. To be a successful information broker, you need solid research skills, computer expertise, and the ability to market yourself. About half of all information brokers are librarians. The rest are experienced in specific subject areas.

A Super Internet Searcher

Fellow information brokers describe Mary Ellen Bates as a super Internet searcher because of her expertise in finding information for businesspeople online. She is the principal and founder of Bates Information Services, one of the leading research and consulting companies in the United States, providing business research and research training services for companies in a diverse array of industries. The company (www.batesinfo.com) also produces a free monthly e-newsletter that offers tips on more efficient researching. Mary Ellen founded her company in 1991 after working as the corporate library manager for MCI Communications

Corporation. She also has held positions as an information specialist for the Federal Judicial Center, the research arm of the federal court system, and as a researcher at a document retrieval company. Besides a bachelor's degree in philosophy, she holds a master's degree in library and information science.

Most of Mary Ellen's time on the job is spent sitting in front of the computer. She uses online databases as well as such resources as trade association and government agency sites on the Internet in her research. Besides reading, she must analyze, synthesize, and package what she has read for her clients. In addition, she has the responsibility of doing all the myriad tasks required to operate a successful business, which takes approximately three hours a day. Part of this time is devoted to marketing activities, participating in e-mail discussion groups, and volunteering for professional associations. Mary Ellen also spends time reading print materials such as the *Wall Street Journal, Wired, Information Advisor,* and *Searcher* magazines, as well as online magazines and a number of professional Listservs to keep current professionally.

Career Advice. In the future, Mary Ellen feels the need for information brokers will accelerate as more and more people discover how difficult it is to access accurate information quickly. She believes prospective information brokers will find courses in business helpful, as they will be running a business. Plus, Mary Ellen advises joining the Association of Independent Information Professionals (www.aiip.org) to gain access to solid advice from those already in this profession.

For Further Reading

So much of research involves reading. Here is a job that truly allows bookworms to combine avocation with vocation. The following books provide additional information on careers in research.

Bates, Mary Ellen, and Reva Basch. *Building and Running a Successful Research Business: A Guide for the Independent Information Professional.* Medford, NJ: Information Today, 2003.

Camenson, Blythe. *Opportunities in Museum Careers.* New York: McGraw-Hill, 2006.

Hock, Randolph. *The Extreme Searcher's Internet Handbook: A Guide for the Serious Searcher.* Medford, NJ: Information Today, 2007.

McGann, James G., and Erik C. Johnson. *Comparative Think Tanks, Politics, and Public Policy.* Northhampton, MA: Edward Elgar Publishing, 2006.

Schlein, Alan M. *Find It Online: The Complete Guide to Online Research*, 4th ed. Tempe, AZ: Facts on Demand Press, 2004.

CHAPTER NINE

Public-Sector Careers

Reading for the Government

W hen bookworms look for jobs that will let them do a lot of reading, one major employer to look at is the government. The federal, state and provincial, and local governments in the United States and Canada actually employ more people than any other employers. These different levels of government were formed to provide public services. We use some of them every day when we drive on roads, listen to weather reports, and buy uncontaminated food and safe medicine. Few people are aware of all the vital services that governments provide. In both countries, the federal government defends us from foreign aggression and terrorism, represents our interests abroad, enforces laws, and administers domestic programs and agencies. Closer to home, state and provincial governments and local governments provide us with such services as transportation, public safety, and education.

Government agencies employ people in occupations that are found in nearly every industry in North America as well as in many jobs that are found only in the public sector. The job opportunities for bookworms are enormous, as federal, state and provincial, and local governments hire thousands of new employees each month, and these jobs offer certain advantages. First of all, public-sector jobs usually offer more long-term job security than typically found in the private sector. And they also typically offer better benefits and inflation protection than jobs in the private sector, and in some areas, better wages. Plus, some jobs offer the chance to work flexible hours as well as in "flexi-place" programs, which allow selected workers to perform some job duties at home or from regional centers. There is also the inviting opportunity to get considerable responsibility early in your career.

Working for the United States Government

Most jobs with the federal government are found in the executive branch, which employs 98 percent of all federal civilian employees (excluding U.S. Postal Service workers). They work in the fifteen executive cabinet departments and nearly ninety independent agencies. Executive branch employees don't just work in Washington, D.C. In fact, close to 90 percent work in other geographical areas, including those who work abroad. What's more, you can often keep the same job and move from state to state or even city to city.

Although people tend to think that the number of people working for the federal government is growing rapidly, this is certainly not true. The period of rapid growth was the 1960s and 1970s. Since then, federal employment has not grown as rapidly as nonfederal employment. In fact, employment is projected to decline by almost 5 percent before 2016. One area that will continue to grow is information analysis, which is good news for bookworms. Overall, many job openings will arise from the need to replace workers who retire or leave the federal government. Competition can be expected to be high for many jobs in times of economic uncertainty.

How to Find Out About Jobs

You can get all the information you need for obtaining a position with the federal government from the Office of Personnel Management through USAJOBS, the government's official employment system. This resource for locating and applying for job opportunities can be accessed through the Internet at www.usajobs.opm.gov. On any given day, you can search the database of more than eighty-five thousand jobs and access a wide range of information about federal agencies. Because agencies do their own hiring and have different requirements, procedures and information required often vary. All require the same basic resume information, but some agencies require additional information. Other sources for job information include newspaper advertisements, a limited number of listings in professional journals, and college placement offices.

How to Get a Job

In order to get the federal job that is right for you, all you have to do is follow three simple steps.

1. Create your account. This lets you create and post resumes, attract employers, and have jobs e-mailed to you.
2. Search for jobs. Search the database and use your resume to apply online instantly.
3. Manage your career. Get all the information and advice you need on obtaining a job in the government.

Whenever you find out about a job opening, get a copy of the vacancy announcement, which provides all the details you need to apply for the job. It provides the identifying number of the particular job, which you must have because the same job title could be found in more than one agency. It lists the deadlines for submitting applications and helpful information on salary, job title, number of positions available, location of the job, job description, and qualifications required.

Besides formally submitting an application for a job, it is also helpful to contact individuals who hire at the agencies that interest you and ask for advice, information, and possible interviews. Another way to get your foot in the door for a job in any branch of the federal government is by obtaining an internship. Not only will you learn firsthand what different government jobs are like, you will also become acquainted with the individuals who are doing the hiring for many positions.

Government Jobs That Pay You to Read

Perhaps one of the hardest things to do is to find out where the best jobs for bookworms are. In general, the occupational groups where you will find these jobs are in the following General Schedule occupational groups:

- GS-0100: social science, psychology, and welfare
- GS-0300: general administrative, clerical, and office services
- GS-1000: information and arts
- GS-1400: library and archives
- GS-1800: investigation group

Jobs that involve doing studies and research—and there are many in these categories within the federal government—are definitely ones that are going to pay you to read. One such job is as a social science analyst. There are thousands of jobs in this category located in different government units throughout the country. Because this position is very desirable, the competition for entry-level positions is keen. Many successful job seekers have master's degrees when only a bachelor's degree is required.

Another area in which bookworms may find jobs is within the intelligence community. This includes the Central Intelligence Agency, the Federal Bureau of Investigation, the Drug Enforcement Agency, and other related agencies. The National Archives, presidential libraries, the Smithsonian Institution, and the National Trust for Historic Preservation are additional places where bookworms should look for jobs in the federal government.

Jobs in the Legislative and Judicial Branches

Although the lion's share of jobs in the federal government is found in agencies of the executive branch, jobs in the legislative and judicial branches are also available. You can find out about some of these jobs by visiting the federal jobs website at www.usajobs.opm.gov. On the legislative side, bookworms are most likely to find appealing jobs at the Government Accountability Office, the Library of Congress, the Congressional Research Service, the Copyright Office, the Government Printing Office, and the Congressional Budget Office.

Jobs with the Congressional Research Service. An excellent place for bookworms to find jobs is in the Congressional Research Service. Hundreds of social science analysts are employed here to give members of Congress and congressional committees information and to make impartial analyses of pending policy issues. Analysts might be assigned to find out what the alternatives are to the current structure of congressional committees or the ways in which affordable housing can best be provided. The analysts do research, compile materials, and gather the pros and cons on an issue. A senior researcher may develop his or her own data. Entire days can be spent doing nothing but on-the-job reading.

Jobs on Capitol Hill. Senators and representatives have offices both in Washington, D.C., and in their home districts. The Washington staffs are larger and, because they have staff members who do research, are better job bets for bookworms. If you want a job with a senator or representative, it doesn't hurt to go to the congressperson's office. There is an unbelievable amount of competition for staff vacancies, and it can be helpful to have made contact with those who do the hiring.

Bookworms can also find jobs on legislative committees and subcommittees that require people with specific knowledge or experience in certain policy areas. Both the House and Senate have websites where you can learn about job vacancies. For additional information, contact:

U.S. House of Representatives
Office of Human Resources
102 Ford House Office Building
Washington, DC 20515
www.house.gov/cao-hr

Senate Placement Office
SH-116 Hart Senate Office Building
Washington, DC 20510
www.senate.gov/employment

Working for the Canadian Government

Similar to the Unites States, the Canadian federal government has three branches: executive, legislative, and judicial. The legislature is made up of an elected House of Commons and an appointed Senate. There are about one hundred distinctly different job titles in the Canadian civil service. The number of employees in the Canadian federal government continues to grow—increasing the job opportunities for bookworms.

The Public Service Commission of Canada offers a website at www.jobs-emplois.gc.ca as your guide to Canadian government jobs. It focuses on the major government agencies that account for most of the government employment in Canada. The website's links take you directly to the job listings and provide you with an overview of the responsibilities of each job, its salary, and the key qualifications required. You will also find out how to apply for the job and where to submit your application. Civil service jobs are typically filled by examination. Each agency administers a different examination for each job. To receive a job offer, you must not only do well on the examination, but you must also do well on all subsequent interviews to receive a job offer.

Working for State and Provincial Governments

There are actually more jobs at the state level than at the federal level in the United States. The same is true for Canada. Many of these jobs in both countries are in higher education and libraries, which are favorite places for bookworms to work. Jobs at the state and provincial level in the executive, legislative, and judicial branches are similar to those in the federal governments but on a smaller scale.

You will find announcements of jobs in state and provincial governments on federal job websites as well as on state and provincial websites. In addition, you will find job announcements in such places as bulletin boards in government buildings, public libraries, and community organizations. After you have found the announcement of a job that appeals to you, follow the instructions on the announcement to submit your application. It is also a good idea to contact the human resources departments within the agencies doing the hiring.

Some State Jobs for Bookworms

Look for jobs for social science analysts because these jobs require considerable reading on the state level just as they do on the federal level. In most states, you will find some of these jobs in legislative auditors' offices. As an analyst, you would determine how well state programs, such as welfare or highway maintenance, are working. Then you would write reports to provide this information for the legislature. Job requirements for this position usually are a master's degree in an area such as public affairs, economics, political science, or one of the social sciences, plus some research experience. You can sometimes get a temporary position on a project that will lead to full-time employment.

Another state job that requires reading is legislative analyst for a house or senate research department. These analysts draft bills and amendments, summarize bills, and do research studies. They apply academic research to public policy. Holders of these jobs have master's degrees or are lawyers. Knowing how to use a computer is essential in all of these jobs.

Working for Local Governments

It is at the local level that you can work most closely with the people. The greatest number of employees in this group is teachers. Finding and getting a job at this level is often a very informal process, especially in very small governmental units. Larger units have personnel departments that post vacancy announcements.

Working as an Elected Official

Some elected officials find themselves absolutely drowning in materials to be read. Most legislators—at all government levels—can never get all the job-related reading done. The president, governors, and mayors of large cities all have so much reading to do that they frequently ask assistants to limit reports to one-page summaries. Judges also must necessarily spend much of their time reading.

A Reader's Career in the Public Sector

Being a curious person who is constantly reading has allowed Carson Ford to hold several excellent jobs in the public sector even though she is not a college graduate. Her career also demonstrates the wide variety of jobs bookworms can find in this arena.

After ten years in advertising, Carson opted to work in the public sector because she wanted a more meaningful job that offered opportunities for personal growth. Her background helped her obtain a job with the state as director of the Soldiers and Sailors Monument Restoration Project in Indianapolis, Indiana. This project required raising $12 million. The lieutenant governor and his office were responsible for raising the corporate dollars, and Carson had the task of raising the grassroots dollars. She decided to get the Indiana schoolchildren involved because all Indiana students throughout the state study Indiana history in the fourth grade. Ball State University faculty helped her develop a curriculum on the history of the monument and the Civil War. The director's job was perfect for a bookworm, as Carson was required to get very involved in reading about the Civil War and the history of the monument in order to raise the money for the restoration. In two years, the fund-raising goal was accomplished.

With her solid experience at the state level, Carson was able to move easily to the local level, becoming the executive director of the Greater Indianapolis Progress Committee, a bipartisan advisory board to the mayor of Indianapolis. Again, Carson was constantly reading on the job to learn more about the issues that would lead to the rebirth of downtown Indianapolis. After six years in this job, Carson became the executive director of the Heartland Film Festival. This was a fun job because her mission was to promote life-affirming films for the Indianapolis festival, which was held once a year for a week in October. It was also a challenging job because she was the first director and had the responsibility of organizing the festival.

After two years with the festival organization, Carson returned to working for the state as director of resource development at the Pleasant Run Children's Home. In this job, she did all the home's marketing and fund-raising. There was also a lot of reading because Carson had to learn about the field of abused and neglected children. Carson feels that some of her best reading was the essays and poems written by the children at the treatment facility during her years in this position. Because reading resources were limited for the children, this bookworm started a library and made sure that every child received a new book for the holidays. She had the children in the program serve as the librarians, cataloging and checking the books in and out.

Continuing in the state government arena, Carson worked as executive director of the Indiana Literacy Foundation. This was the perfect job for a reader because it required her to spend much of her day reading as she sought funding to support the program. Appropriately, this is also a job in which she promoted reading. Carson says that she could not have handled this part of the job unless she herself was a reader. Reading is such a way of life for her that off the job she is always reading nonfiction, fiction, and history books.

For Further Reading

Bookworms who want to find government jobs that let them read will find the task much easier if they learn more about the process. It is also absolutely essential to have an understanding of how governments work. You need to read books like the following, which provide information about the government and governmental jobs.

United States

Damp, Dennis V. *The Book of U.S. Government Jobs: Where They Are, What's Available, and How to Get One.* McKees Rock, PA: Bookhaven Press, 2008.

JIST Editors. *Guide to America's Federal Jobs: A Complete Directory of Federal Career Opportunities.* Indianapolis, IN: JIST Works, 2005.

Mannion, James. *The Everything Guide to Government Jobs: A Complete Handbook to Hundreds of Lucrative Opportunities Across the Nation.* Cincinnati, OH: Adams Media Corporation, 2007.

Troutman, Kathryn Kraemer. *Federal Resume Guidebook,* 3rd ed. Indianapolis, IN: JIST Works, 2004.

Canada

Bernier, Luc, Keith Brownsey, and Michael Howlett, eds. *Executive Styles in Canada: Cabinet Structures and Leadership Practices in Canadian Government.* Toronto: University of Toronto Press, 2005.

Malcolmson, Patrick, and Richard Myers. *The Canadian Regime: An Introduction to Parliamentary Government in Canada,* 3rd ed. Peterborough, ON: Broadview Press, 2005.

CHAPTER TEN

Private-Sector Careers

Reading for Businesses

Although the federal governments of the United States and Canada are the largest single employers in North America, it is the private sector where most of the jobs are. These jobs are scattered across the continent, from the smallest of towns with fewer than fifty people to megalopolises with millions of inhabitants. What is fascinating about jobs in the private sector is that they range from the traditional jobs that we all are familiar with to new jobs that didn't exist just a few years ago. Many of these new jobs are associated with the creative use of our constantly expanding technology.

Where you are able to find employment in the private sector is affected by the state of the economy. Some occupations are relatively recession proof. Others fluctuate with consumer demand. One thing is certain: education will pay dividends in finding a job in the private sector in the future. The fastest-growing job areas are those that require employees to have associate's or bachelor's degrees. You have already read about careers in publishing, education, research, and glamour industries. Now, you will find out about the professional and business jobs that should be filled by people who love to read.

With the constant explosion of new technology and knowledge in almost every field, few employees can afford not to read to keep up with what is happening in their areas of employment. The secret is to find the jobs that require more than routine reading. Quite often these jobs are to be found in areas where research is done.

If a bookworm has a specific field of interest, it may be possible to turn this interest into a job asset. The reader who has developed an in-depth knowledge of an industry, a country, or a product is a more attractive candidate for a job than someone who will have to learn vital background information on the job.

Reading Jobs in Traditional Professions

Occupations that require advanced education and training and also involve intellectual skills—such as medicine, law, engineering, theology, and teaching—are regarded as professions. If you have an intense interest in one of these professions, it is possible to find a job within it that lets you read. Because many professions allow one to be self-employed, you can also tailor your job to fit your love of reading.

Doctors Read

Doctors who teach and those who work at research institutions spend much of their time reading—not only to increase understanding, but also in order to write papers. Even a doctor who primarily treats patients finds it essential to do at least four or five hours a week of solid professional reading beyond the routine reading of charts.

Lawyers Read

The younger lawyers are, the more they read because they need to do more research. It is not unusual for a junior attorney in a law firm to spend three or four hours a day reading briefs and cases. In addition, law clerks for judges, especially appellate judges, do a lot of reading. As lawyers become more senior, their reading time decreases. Still, most read for one or two hours a day, and it is not unusual for them to read three or more. Nowadays, more and more of this reading is done on computers rather than in law books because information can be accessed faster in this way.

Lawyers do not just practice law. One job that requires a legal background as well as very intense reading is putting headnotes on cases for publishers of law books. Another job is as a teacher in a law school.

Engineers Read

A career as an engineer could be in any one of twenty-five major specialties, which are further divided into numerous subdivisions. Engineers must read to keep abreast of the latest scientific discoveries in their fields because engineers are often the link between scientific discoveries and their applications. They must learn about such things as the development of new and improved materials in order to design and build machinery, roads, bridges, power plants, cars, factories, and products. While their reading is concentrated on technical journals, engineers must also read to learn about governmental regulations affecting their work, especially in the area of environmental concerns.

Members of the Clergy Read

Reading for members of the clergy can be for contemplation, gathering information for sermons, learning more about one's faith, and increasing knowledge in an area like counseling.

Stockbrokers and Financial Analysts Read

When people buy stocks and bonds (securities), they usually deal with stockbrokers. Because things are always changing so fast in these markets, brokers have to snatch every moment they can to keep up with what is happening. Unfortunately, not too much of this can take place during the day when the market is open and they are busy dealing with clients. Also, because they receive reams of material to digest, stockbrokers must skim much of what they read.

If you are fascinated by what is happening in the securities market, there are analyst jobs in the investment area that are made just for bookworms. On the sell side, the jobs are with brokerage firms and investment banks that sell securities to investors; on the buy side, the jobs are with bank trust departments, insurance companies, and fund management firms.

On the sell side, analysts focus on areas such as faster transaction processing, trade execution, and global fulfillment for their firms' clients. On the buy side, analysts spend their time figuring out what should be bought and sold for their firms' portfolios. On either side, knowledge increases the probability that a decision will be a correct one.

Analysts read constantly to stay up-to-date with what is happening because things change every day. Stocks and bonds that appear to be an excellent investment at the start of the week may be a poor choice by the end of the week.

Most analysts are assigned a specific industry. Within that area, they will read all the information that they can get their hands on about the industry, firms in the industry, related government regulations, and world events that may affect the industry. Weather, revolutions, and governmental policy changes are just a few of the events that can change the value of securities. Besides reading, much time is spent talking to people to find out what is happening. After gathering information, analysts write reports to share that information.

If you decide to work as an analyst in the securities industry, you are likely to be working in New York City in the United States—the financial headquarters for more firms than any other place—or in Toronto—the financial center of Canada. It is important for you to know that employment in these firms is very cyclical. When times are good, employment is up. After contractions in the market, the number of employees is quickly reduced.

There is a very high level of competition for positions as analysts in the securities industry. It is possible for recent college graduates to enter this field and learn on the job. However, senior analysts usually have master's degrees in business. More and more also have attained the professional designation of Chartered Financial Analyst (CFA), which is obtained after passing a series of three tests and showing experience in the field.

Bank Economists Read

Like stockbrokers and financial analysts, the management team at a bank needs to know what is happening around the world in the economy. At banks that have $10 billion or more in deposits, there are staff economists. The chief economist is likely to have a doctorate in economics. Assistants probably also have advanced degrees. However, there are entry-level jobs for college graduates with majors in economics. At all levels, economists read so they can write reports on the economy for the bank and its clients.

Political Analysts Read

Julie Sedky reads from 40 to 50 percent of her time on the job as a political analyst at a firm that does public policy research for institutional investors. She tries to anticipate and analyze changes in governmental policy that will affect her clients, who invest other people's money and don't want to be surprised by what happens in Washington, D.C. She regularly reads such publications as the *Washington Post, Wall Street Journal, Bureau of National Affairs Daily Report for Executives, Congressional Quarterly,* and the *Economist,* as well as excerpts from the *Congressional Record,* materials put out by the Congressional Budget Office and congressional leaders, and a number of private newsletters that tell what's going on in Washington, D.C. Julie's expertise in finding information is such that she sometimes finds her own words in references.

Jobs for Consultants

Consultants act as problem solvers in both the public and private sectors. They are also hired to do work similar to that done in think tanks.

Being a consultant means doing research and analysis for a client. It could involve determining how a scarcity of labor would affect a firm. It might be a question of identifying the major trends in an industry. No matter what the task, the major tool for accomplishing it is always reading.

While consulting firms vary in size from one-person operations to large international corporations, it is at the larger firms that most entry-level positions are found. Recent college graduates can often find jobs as assistants on projects.

Jobs in Corporate America

The companies that make automobiles, soap, frozen dinners, and paper, as well as the companies that drill for oil or build airplanes, have jobs for bookworms. No matter what it produces, if the company is large enough, there will be jobs that require reading. When you look for a job in corporate America, be sure to investigate areas such as human resources, marketing, and consumer relations.

Human Resources Employees Read

All the hiring and firing of employees, the negotiating of labor agreements, and the determining of benefits and salaries are done in the human resources department at a large company. This is the department that deals with all the people who work at a company. Because the federal government as well as state and provincial governments have many laws that spell out exactly how employees are to be treated, employees in this department must do a lot of reading just to keep up with statutory requirements. Then they must make sure that the people in operations know what these laws are and follow them.

Terri Nelson works for a Fortune 500 company as a placement specialist. This is not a job that you can just step into because so many companies want college graduates who have experience, and there are few training positions. Many placement specialists begin as clerical workers to get basic business experience. Terri, who has a college degree, worked as a secretary in human resources, a bookkeeper, and a customer service representative before becoming a placement specialist.

During a typical week, Terri may read as many as five hundred resumes of people seeking employment with her company. She is looking for people who meet the qualifications for positions that are available. She reviews the resumes of all the qualified candidates for a position and then writes down questions to ask each of these applicants. She also interviews applicants and conducts an orientation program for new employees.

Terri estimates that she reads 70 to 80 percent of her time on the job. Besides reading resumes, she keeps up with the literature in her field and reads government rulings.

Market Developers Read

In his career in market development for a television network, Michael Sanchez and his team members negotiate agreements with hundreds of cable and satellite providers and develop marketing initiatives to promote products and services for the network and its affiliates. It is extremely helpful that Michael has always loved to read because he probably spends five hours a day reading on the job. Although this is not reading the novels that he loves, his ability to read fast to absorb information about past and current business relationships has contributed to his own success as well as the continued success of his company.

Michael explains that it is imperative for him to read on the job because the television network business is always changing—new technologies, new partners, and new competitors. He points out that reading is especially critical when it comes to contracts. When he says "reading," it sometimes means reading the same contract over and over and over! The words don't change, but his interpretation just might. During a typical day on the job, he reads forty or fifty e-mails, two newspapers, and the trade publications in his career area (*Variety, Multichannel News, CableFAX*), along with some news and entertainment magazines and four or five contracts or reports.

Marketing Researchers Read

Some companies use information services to find out about marketing trends or how consumers like a product. Other companies have their own marketing research departments and may also use information services. Jobs in marketing research involve keeping in touch with what consumers want through test marketing and product testing. This includes collecting data through research and reading. The background needed for this job varies from company to company. Many marketing researchers have a bachelor's degree in business and an advanced degree in marketing, finance, or accounting.

Consumer Relations Workers Read

When consumers are unhappy, they write to companies to voice their complaints. Companies receive mail asking why a prize was not included in a cereal box as promised or complaining that a new car has needed numerous adjustments. Companies also receive mail asking for information about such things as products or company activities. Letters may ask why a product isn't biodegradable or why a company is doing business with a certain country.

To keep their customers' goodwill, employees in customer relations departments answer all of these letters. Some employees read and answer mail all day, while others alternate between handling mail and fielding telephone calls. Many letters can be answered with personalized form letters. Answering some letters requires research. Companies try to answer every letter as accurately as possible.

To get a job answering mail or the telephone, it is not always necessary to have a college degree. In addition, this is a job where experience is not required, but employees do have to demonstrate an ability to write.

For Further Reading

Because the private sector is where nine out of ten jobs are in North America, this is the area where bookworms should do the most reading. Investigate what careers in different professions offer as well as what jobs with financial institutions are like. Finally, read to find out what jobs are available in corporate America. Reading the following books is just a starting point for learning about jobs in the private sector.

Careers in Focus: Business, 2nd ed. New York: Facts on File, 2005.

Farr, Michael, and Marie A. Pavlicko. *Young Person's Guide to Getting and Keeping a Good Job*, 3rd ed. Indianapolis, IN: JIST Works, 2006.

Hamadeh, Samer, and Mark Oldman. *Vault Guide to Top Internships*. New York: Vault, Inc., 2007.

Stair, Lila B., and Leslie Stair. *Careers in Business*. New York: McGraw-Hill, 2005.

U.S. Department of Labor. *Top 300 Careers: Your Complete Guidebook to Major Jobs in Every Field*. Indianapolis, IN: JIST Works, 2006.

CHAPTER ELEVEN

Even More Careers for Bookworms

Seeing Endless Opportunities

If you haven't found a job yet that truly intrigues you because it lets you do a lot of reading, read on. Doing some additional reading will lead you to even more careers. Browse through an occupational handbook or jobs guide while thinking of your fondness for reading as well as your interests and skills to discover more possibilities. Expand your options further by reading want ads in newspapers and professional journals and visiting online job sites. Use a search engine to find additional "reading" job possibilities. Remember, it may take some creativity to find a job that matches your interests and abilities. In the meantime, you may even want to volunteer for an organization that promotes literacy to satisfy your need to be associated with reading. Here are a few more careers that other bookworms have found to be quite satisfying.

Essay Reviewer

Just think of the tens of thousands of high school students who take the SAT or the ACT tests for college admission and have to write essays as part of these tests. And these aren't the only tests where essays need to be read and scored. The list gets longer each year and includes advance placement (AP) tests, achievement tests, and tests for teacher certification. For most tests, each essay has to be read and scored by two readers following a scoring criteria established by the test publisher. If there is a certain discrepancy between the scores, a third reader also reads an essay. Some training is required for this work, but it very definitely is a job that involves reading 100 percent of the time. What is excellent about this job is that it is a paid position (hourly) that you can frequently do from your own home if you have the necessary computer and Internet access. To get one of these jobs, you will probably need a bachelor's degree or higher and may need experience teaching a high school or college-level course that requires writing.

Translator

A good translator needs to be able to change the written word from one language to another. In order to do this, a translator really needs to be a bookworm in two languages. Translators are especially in demand in businesses, government agencies, and research organizations. Many also freelance or work for translation services. This is a job that offers both full-time and part-time employment. Bookworms in this field need to be prepared to read all kinds of scientific, technical, commercial, and legal material.

Braille Transcriber

You will not get rich being a braille transcriber, but you will be providing a very important service to blind people who read braille. Braille transcribers turn the printed word on all kinds of subjects into braille. This can be done by using six of the regular keys and the function keys on a computer or less commonly by using a device called a braillewriter. Braille transcribing also can be done by just typing exact copy and using special computer programs. However, a trained braillist must know how to format the copy correctly in braille.

To become truly proficient in transcribing braille can take several years. Most transcribers take a class so they can become certified by the Library of Congress. To gain certification, you must submit an almost perfect forty-page document in braille. You can find jobs as a braille transcriber with braille book publishers and state departments of education. Most of this work is done on a freelance basis, so you can work at home. School districts also have jobs for transcribers that involve visiting schools and preparing teacher handouts and quizzes for those students who need the work in braille. Furthermore, there are many opportunities to transcribe braille as a volunteer.

Audiobook Reader

If you have an excellent reading voice, you may be able to find a job that pays you for reading aloud. As you have probably noticed, more and more people are listening to recorded books in all types of places, from their cars to jogging paths. People who make these recordings can earn hundreds of dollars a day. The problem is that obtaining one of these jobs is extremely difficult. Many readers are professional actors and broadcasters. Furthermore, recording studios are generally located only in metropolitan areas.

Genealogist

People want to know where their great-grandmothers were born and what their great-great-grandfathers did for a living. Genealogists help people learn about their ancestors. They research for clues in libraries, church records, courthouses, old letters, diaries, newspaper clippings, census records, and government archives. Much of the work can be done online. This job requires keeping careful records. It also requires people who like to work alone; most genealogists are self-employed. There are no formal educational requirements for becoming a genealogist. Although there are some courses in genealogy that can be helpful, most people acquire job knowledge through other genealogists and reading material on genealogy.

. . . .

Abstractor

If you enjoy independent research and doing very exacting work, you might like to be an abstractor for an abstract or title insurance company. This work involves finding all the records on a piece of property so that a clear title can be issued when the property is sold. Abstractors search through dusty volumes in the basements of courthouses and also use computers to find this information. They never stop reading all day long. Although you don't need a college education to be an abstractor, some courses in law, real estate, and business can be helpful. It takes from four to six years of on-the-job training to learn how to do all kinds of abstracts. Most abstractors work in metropolitan areas, where there are usually job openings for this position.

. . . .

Accountant

You may think accountants are just numbers people. Nevertheless, this is also a job that requires considerable reading. Tax accountants must be up-to-date on the thousands of pages of federal and state and provincial regulations. Internal auditors have to make sure that companies are following corporate policies and government regulations. Plus, most states and provinces require public accountants to take continuing education courses.

. . . .

Word Processor

Word processing can just be transcribing work and putting it into an attractive format. Or it can involve editing and revising letters, reports, and other printed materials. Although it is a job that involves considerable reading, it is essentially clerical in nature. One advantage of this job is the possibility of doing it from your home as a telecommuter.

Nutritionist

Nutritionists and dietitians plan food and nutrition programs in many settings, from hospitals to schools to doctors' offices. Because the information on nutrition is constantly growing, they must do a lot of reading to meet the nutritional needs of those they serve. Lisa Mahan is a nutrition coordinator for a large cardiology practice. Her patients rely on her to sort through all the information published on diet and health so that she can tell them what is appropriate for them. Lisa says that she is always reading on the job, whether it is patient charts, online materials, books, journals, newsletters, or health magazines.

Judge

Television has brought judges and their work into your home. Outside of the courtroom, judges must spend considerable time reading documents on pleadings and motions. They also have to research legal issues. The amount of reading judges do varies by jurisdiction. General trial judges do not do as much reading as federal and state appellate court judges, who study lower-court decisions to see if they should be upheld or overturned.

Wire Editor

If you are curious about what is happening in Australia, South Dakota, and every corner of the world, being an editor for a news agency that distributes news and photographs to newspapers, radio and television stations, newsmagazines, and online media is a good choice. These editors sit in front of a computer screen and read news. They pull copy and edit it and also route copy to clients. It is a job that lets you read for almost eight hours a day and also puts the news of the world at your fingertips.

Author

Without authors, there would be no books, magazines, textbooks, newsletters, pamphlets, bulletins, newspapers, or online materials for bookworms to read. Authors aren't just writers; most are bookworms, too. Think of all the research that has to be done by authors. Imagine how much reading James Michener had to do in order to write *Hawaii* or *Centennial*. Consider how much reading was done to write this book.

And don't forget the tremendous amount of reading that authors of textbooks do. Indeed, being an author is a superb career for bookworms and other literary types. While the majority of aspiring writers may never get their books published by traditional publishing houses, they can now get their books published by on-demand publishers. What's appealing about this is that these publishers only produce books after they've been ordered and paid for.

Volunteering Opportunities for Bookworms

Volunteering provides an unpaid opportunity for bookworms to do additional reading. Libraries and schools need volunteers to help nurture the love of reading in children by reading to them. Schools and literacy programs need volunteers to tutor children and adults who need help in learning to read. The biggest reward from such volunteering lies in bringing the joy of reading to others.

Recorder for the Blind and Dyslexic

Making recordings for the blind and dyslexic can be a very satisfying activity for bookworms of all ages. Several organizations can give you information about making these recordings. One organization is Recording for the Blind & Dyslexic. For more information, contact:

Recording for the Blind & Dyslexic
20 Roszel Road
Princeton, NJ 08540
www.rfbd.org

You will need to pass a vocal test to become a volunteer. Your first task will be to learn how to interpret all the marks so you will know how to read the text. Volunteers are then required to read at least two hours a week, usually reading textbooks. If you are reading textbooks in subject areas such as calculus and chemistry, you will need to be knowledgeable about the subject in order to explain the illustrations and symbols used in these books.

Still More Career Options

The more you think about the different kinds of material that people read, the longer your list of careers for bookworms will become. There are people who create crossword puzzles and people who make all kinds of tests, from achievement tests to intelligence tests. Then there are people who clip what others have written for clipping services. Be sure to talk to fellow bookworms about the careers that they have found that let them read on the job.

The Future for Bookworms

The future is bright for bookworms and other literary types seeking jobs that allow them to be paid for reading. Tomorrow's best jobs will be in areas that require education, and, as a group, bookworms tend to be well educated. They can be part of the limelight as they search for the perfect scripts for movies and TV shows. They can face challenges as they search for answers to perplexing societal questions. They can find jobs close to books in libraries. They can start their own companies with the goal of making reading more enjoyable in some way for others. And they will find a bonanza of reading jobs within the rapidly growing information services industry.

The years ahead should offer bookworms more and more opportunities to combine avocation and vocation because the world is deluged with an ever-increasing volume of written and online information, which will increase the need for reading on the job. Bookworms can also anticipate that reading on the job will continue to mean doing more and more reading on computer screens. The future presents opportunities to do more reading in just about every career.

About the Authors

....

Marjorie Eberts and Margaret Gisler have been writing together professionally for thirty-one years. They are prolific freelance authors with more than ninety books in print. Their publications include more than twenty career books, language arts and mathematics textbooks, advice books for parents, and children's books. Besides writing books, the two authors write the King Features syndicated "Dear Teacher" column that appears in newspapers throughout the country.

Writing this book was a special pleasure for Eberts and Gisler because they are decidedly bookworms. Investigating the many careers that require reading on the job let them spend hours reading—their favorite avocation. It also gave them the opportunity to talk to fellow bookworms and learn more about their fascinating careers.

Marjorie Eberts has bachelor's and master's degrees from Stanford University, and Margaret Gisler has her bachelor's and doctoral degrees from Ball State University and her master's from Butler University. Both received their specialist degrees in education from Butler University.